THE 20 MINUTE Piano WORKOUT

By Douglas Riva

D1289189

© Copyright 1987 Ekay Music, Inc., 223 Katonah Avenue, Katonah, NY 10536

Introduction

ALL PIANISTS—from the struggling beginner to the experienced artist—want more technique. We all want to be able to play with greater accuracy, control and apparent ease. The Drills or Etudes included in the *Twenty Minute Workout* have all been written, selected or arranged to help you work toward that goal.

Although developing a fine piano technique is a life-long study, involving years of hard work in isolating and continuously improving the elements that constitute a good technique, the *Twenty Minute Workout* can be of enormous help toward that goal for those without sufficient practice time. Organized into 20 Weeks (or chapters), each week is devoted to different aspects or problems of piano playing—5-finger patterns, chords, double notes, repeated notes, octaves, and more. After completing each Week in the *Twenty Minute Workout* you will also receive a performable piece which contains some of the technical difficulties encountered in the drills . . . a way of enjoying your new found level of facility! Aside from improving your technique, the course will also help your sight-reading to improve.

Each Week or Chapter is accompanied by a Practice Calendar to help you organize your practice time. If you are using the book under a teacher's guidance, follow your teacher's advice. If you study alone, follow the Practice Calendar and your own musical instincts. Try to make the most of each 20 minute period, and do not expect too much of yourself in just one or two sessions. Patient practice will create results!

There are probably as many philosophies of technique as there are pianists. No matter which philosophy or combination of methods you use, the *Twenty Minute Workout* should be able to help you develop your approach. Probably every pianist would agree that developing your technique is not a mindless, mechanical activity. It is not merely a physical exercise. It requires your full and complete attention to achieve the most musical results possible.

As you practice, aim to produce the best tone. Do not exaggerate motions—use only the amount of energy necessary to produce the musical effect you want. Pain is the body's way of telling us that we are doing something wrong. If you feel pain, stop and try to analyze what you are doing that causes pain.

When you have completed the *Twenty Minute Workout* you will not have developed all the technique you will ever want, but you will certainly have improved your playing, and you will be more prepared to tackle new and more difficult music. GOOD LUCK!

DOUGLAS RIVA *received his musical education at the Juilliard School in New York and at the Academia Marshall in Barcelona. His most important teachers were Eugene List and Mercè Roldós. In 1982, he was invited by the Town Hall Foundation to make his New York debut at Town Hall, performing Granados' Goyescas. Two years later he presented the World Premiere of unknown and unpublished works by Granados in Barcelona, at the request of the composer's daughter.*

Dr. Riva has recorded for Radio WQXR-New York, WXTV-New York and the Voice of America in the United States, and for Radio Nacional de España, Catalunya Radio, TV-3, Radio Miramar and Radio Ser in Spain. He is an Associate Professor at Pace University and the Hoff-Barthelson Music School, and he has lectured at Harvard University, New York University, the New School and Wells College. He is a Contributing Editor of Keyboard Classics, and his recordings have been released by the Musical Heritage Society and the Keystone Music Roll Company.

WEEK
1

Monday	Drill A, First Reading, 5 Minutes Drill A, Second Reading, 5 Minutes Drill B, First Reading, 5 Minutes Drill B, Second Reading, 5 Minutes
Tuesday	Drill C, First Reading, 5 Minutes Drill C, Second Reading, 5 Minutes Drill A, Third Reading, 10 Minutes
Wednesday	Drill C, Third Reading, 10 Minutes Drill B, Third Reading, 5 Minutes Drill A, Third Reading, 5 Minutes
Thursday	Drill A, Fourth Reading, 5 Minutes Drill B, Third Reading, 5 Minutes Drill C, Third Reading, 10 Minutes
Friday	Drill C, Fourth Reading, 5 Minutes Drill C, Fifth Reading, 5 Minutes Drill B, Fourth Reading, 5 Minutes Drill A, Fifth Reading, 5 Minutes
Sat/Sun	Drill A, Sixth Reading, 8 Minutes Drill B, Fourth Reading, 4 Minutes Drill C, Sixth Reading, 8 Minutes

"Warming Up"

EVERY practice session should begin with a warm-up. The following Drill is an excellent one to help you achieve the smoothest sound possible. All of the notes should match in dynamic level (sounding without any accents). Work to achieve control, not speed.

The metronome markings given below, and throughout the TWENTY-MINUTE WORKOUT are intended as a guide. They may be too slow or too fast for you. Pick a tempo that is fast enough to be challenging, but slow enough for you to have complete control over each note.

First Reading
Right hand alone. Play legato (smooth and connected) and *mf* (mezzo forte — moderately loud). ♪=120-144 (♩=60-72).

Second Reading
Left hand alone. Play legato and *mf.* ♪=120-144 (♩=60-72).

Third Reading
Hands together. Play legato and *mf.* ♪=120-144 (♩=60-72).

Fourth Reading
Hands together. Play staccato (short and separated) and *p* (piano—soft). Move each hand up one octave. ♪=152-176 (♩=76-88).

Fifth Reading
Hands together. Play legato and *p.* Move the right hand up one octave and move the left hand down one octave. ♪=176-200 (♩=88-100).

Sixth Reading
Hands together. Play staccato and *f* (forte—loud). Move the right hand up two octaves and move the left hand down two octaves. ♩=104-120.

Drill A

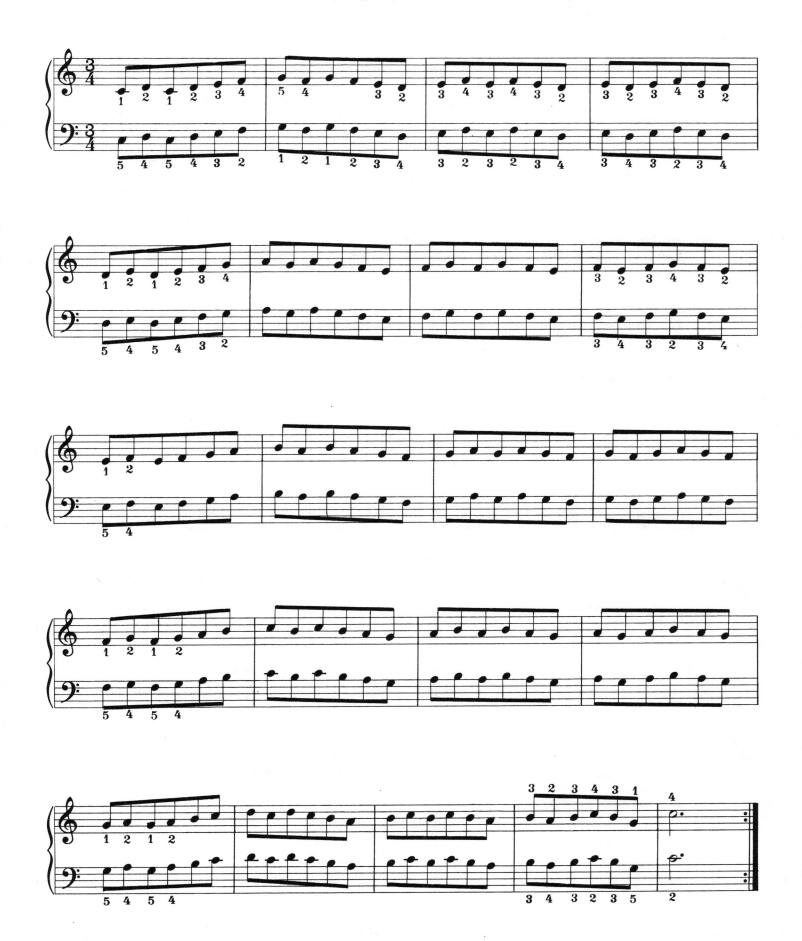

"Left Alone"

THE ABILITY to write with your left hand is no advantage in piano playing. Every pianist has some difficulty making the left hand perform as easily as the right. (Since most music is written with a major portion of the difficulties placed in the right hand, our right hands receive more training than our left hands.) For this reason, the TWENTY-MINUTE WORKOUT contains many Drills for the left hand alone.

First Reading
    Left hand alone. Play legato (smooth and connected) and *p* (piano — soft), ♪=144-168 (♩=72-84).

Second Reading
    Left hand alone. Play staccato (short and separated) and *f* (forte — loud). ♪=176-192 (♩=88-96).

Third Reading
    Left hand alone. Play legato and *f.* Move the hand down one octave. ♩=100-108.

Fourth Reading
    Left hand alone. Play staccato and *p.* Move the hand up one octave. ♩=112-126.

DRILL B

"On The 'A' Train"

THIS STUDY is a more complicated version of Drill A. Like Drill A, this drill will be practiced with variations.

First Reading

Right hand alone. Play legato (smooth and connected) and *mp* (mezzo piano—moderately soft). ♪=120-144 (♩=60-72).

Second Reading

Left hand alone. Play legato and *mp.* ♪=120-144 (♩=60-72).

Third Reading

Hands together. Play legato and *mp.* ♪=120-144 (♩=60-72).

Fourth Reading

Hands together. Play staccato (short and separated) and *p* (piano—soft). Move each hand up one octave. ♪=152-176 (♩=76-88).

Fifth Reading

Hands together. Play legato and *f* (forte—loud). Move the right hand up one octave and move the left hand down one octave. ♪=176-200 (♩=88-100).

Sixth Reading

Hands together. Play staccato and *f.* Move the right hand up two octaves and move the left hand down two octaves. ♩=104-120.

(Drill on next page)

Drill C

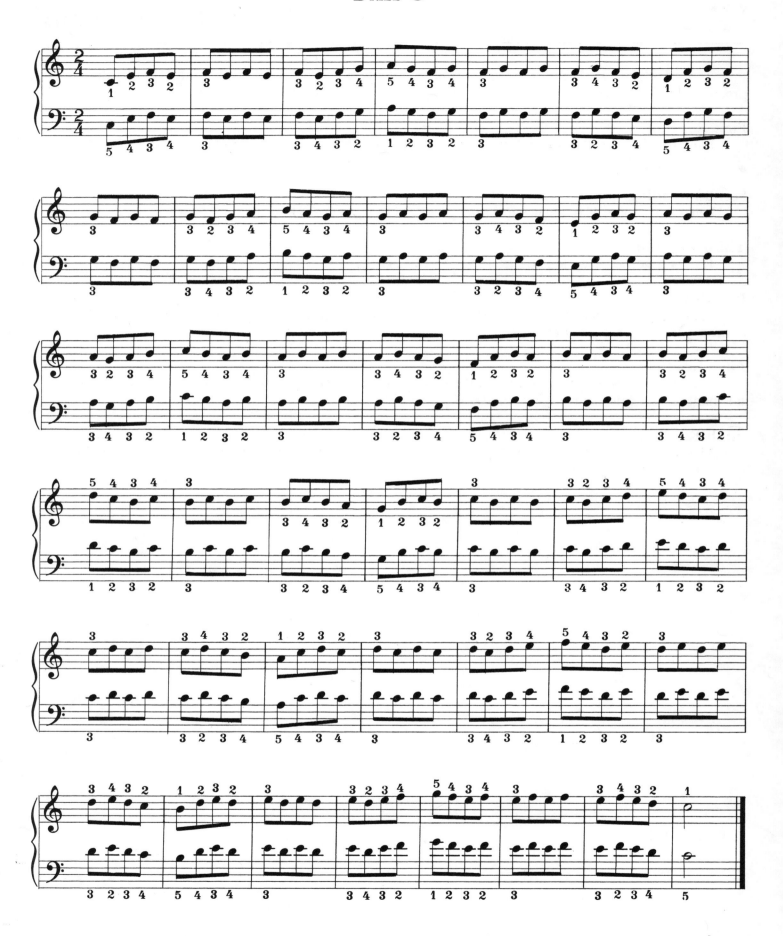

The Flute And The Droome

WILLIAM BYRD

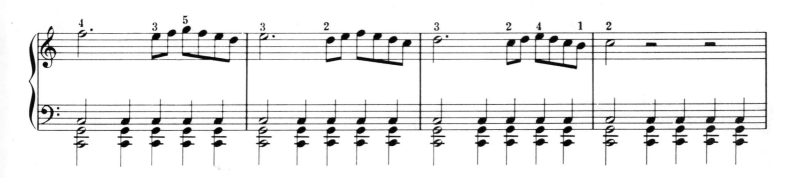

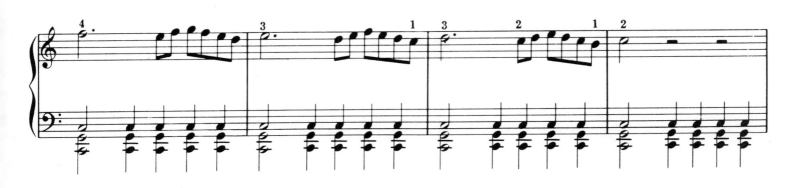

(continued on next page)

Week 2

Monday	Drill A, First Reading, 5 Minutes Drill A, Second Reading, 5 Minutes Drill B, First Reading, 5 Minutes Drill B, Second Reading, 5 Minutes
Tuesday	Drill A, Third Reading, 5 Minutes Drill B, Third Reading, 5 Minutes Drill C, First Reading, 10 Minutes
Wednesday	Drill C, Second Reading, 5 Minutes Drill B, Third Reading, 5 Minutes Drill B, Fourth Reading, 5 Minutes Drill A, Third Reading, 5 Minutes
Thursday	Drill A, Third Reading, 5 Minutes Drill A, Fourth Reading, 5 Minutes Drill C, Third Reading, 5 Minutes Drill B, Fourth Reading, 5 Minutes
Friday	Drill B, Fifth Reading, 5 Minutes Drill C, Fourth Reading, 5 Minutes Drill A, Fifth Reading, 5 Minutes Drill A, Sixth Reading, 5 Minutes
Sat/Sun	Drill C, Fifth Reading, 5 Minutes Drill B, Fifth Reading, 5 Minutes Drill B, Sixth Reading, 5 Minutes Drill A, Sixth Reading, 5 Minutes

"Five Alive"

ALTHOUGH this drill is made up entirely of five-finger patterns, the individual patterns differ from each other. Some of the patterns are on white keys (measures 1-4, for example) while some are on black keys (measures 5-8). When you play on the white keys, with the thumb on a white key, play toward the outer edge of the key. When playing on the black keys, with the thumb on a black key, play toward the cover of the keyboard.

First Reading

Right hand alone. Play legato (smooth and connected) and *p* (piano — soft). ♪=120-144.

Second Reading

Left hand alone. Play legato and *p.* ♪=120-144.

Third Reading

Hands together. Play legato and *p.* ♪=120-144.

Fourth Reading

Hands together. Play legato and *f* (forte — loud). ♪=160-184 (♩=80-92).

Fifth Reading

Hands together. Play staccato (short and separated) and *p.* ♩=80-92.

Sixth Reading

Hands together. Move both hands down one octave. Play staccato and *f.* Increase the tempo to ♩=112-126.

Drill A

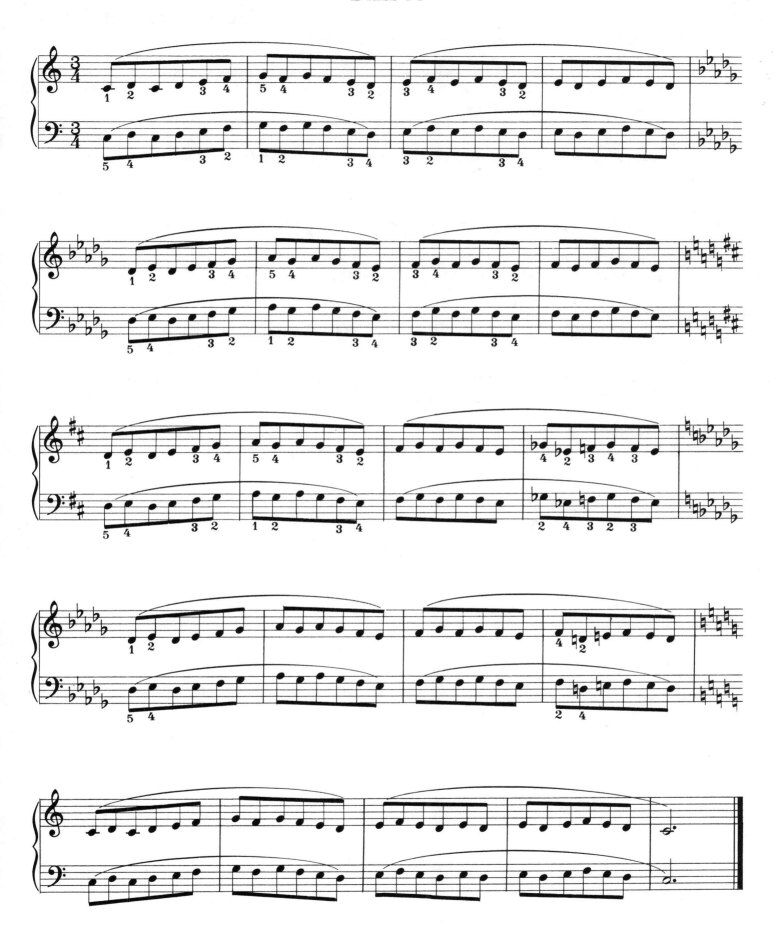

15

"Stretching Out"

WRITTEN by Robert Schumann's father-in-law, Frederick Wieck, this drill concentrates on five-finger patterns with the addition of extensions (stretches) between the thumb and second fingers and between the fourth and fifth fingers.

First Reading

Right hand alone. Play legato (smooth and connected) and *mf* (mezzo forte—moderately loud). ♪=120-144 (♩=60-72).

Second Reading

Left hand alone. Play legato and *mf.* ♪=120-144 (♩=60-72).

Third Reading

Hands together. Play legato and *mf.* ♪=120-144 (♩=60-72).

Fourth Reading

Hands together. Play staccato (short and separated) and *f* (forte — loud). ♩=80-92.

Fifth Reading

Hands together. Move the right hand up one octave. Move the left hand down one octave. Play staccato and *p* (piano — soft). ♩=96-112.

Sixth Reading

Hands together. Play as written. Play legato and *mf.* ♩=116-132.

Drill B

"On The Edge"

WHEN the fifth finger of either hand plays a white key, we naturally play on the outside of the key. But, when the fifth finger is placed on a black key, we must move the arm closer to the piano in order to play on the edge of the black key. As an example, look at measures 1, 2, 4 and 5.

First Reading
Play legato (smooth and connected) and *p* (piano — soft). ♪=120-144 (♩=60-72).

Second Reading
Play staccato (short and separated) and *f* (forte — loud). ♪=120-144 (♩=60-72).

Third Reading
Move the hand up one octave. Play legato and *p.* ♩=76-88.

Fourth Reading
Move the hand down one octave. Play staccato and *p.* ♩=96-108.

Fifth Reading
Play as written, legato and *f.* ♩=112-126.

DRILL C

Jefferson Hornpipe

James Hewitt

WEEK
3

Monday	Drill A, First Reading, 5 Minutes Drill B, First Reading, 5 Minutes Drill B, Second Reading, 5 Minutes Drill C, First Reading, 5 Minutes
Tuesday	Drill C, Second Reading, 5 Minutes Drill C, Third Reading, 5 Minutes Drill A, Second Reading, 5 Minutes Drill B, Third Reading, 5 Minutes
Wednesday	Drill B, Third Reading, 5 Minutes Drill B, Fourth Reading, 5 Minutes Drill C, Fourth Reading, 5 Minutes Drill C, Fifth Reading, 5 Minutes
Thursday	Drill A, Third Reading, 5 Minutes Drill B, Fifth Reading, 5 Minutes Drill C, Fourth Reading, 5 Minutes Drill C, Fifth Reading, 5 Minutes
Friday	Drill C, Sixth Reading, 5 Minutes Drill C, Seventh Reading, 5 Minutes Drill A, Fourth Reading, 5 Minutes Drill B, Sixth Reading, 5 Minutes
Sat/Sun	Drill C, Seventh Reading, 10 Minutes Drill A, Fifth Reading, 5 Minutes Drill B, Sixth Reading, 5 Minutes

"Connections"

AT FIRST GLANCE this drill appears quite easy, but the difficulty of connecting the two hands is obvious as soon as you begin to play. Try to make the music like a continuous chain of sound. Be especially careful to not lift the thumb of the left hand, which is the last note of the left hand passage (the second eighth note in each beat), until you play the first note of the right hand (the first eighth note of the second beat).

First Reading
Hands together. Play legato (smooth and connected) and *mf* (mezzo forte—moderately loud). ♪=126-144.

Second Reading
Hands together. Play legato and *p* (piano—soft). ♪=152-184.

Third Reading
Hands together. Play legato and *f* (forte—loud). ♩=80-92.

Fourth Reading
Hands together. Play legato and *mp* (mezzo piano—moderately soft). ♩=96-116.

Fifth Reading
Hands together. Play legato and *mp*. ♩=120-138.

DRILL A

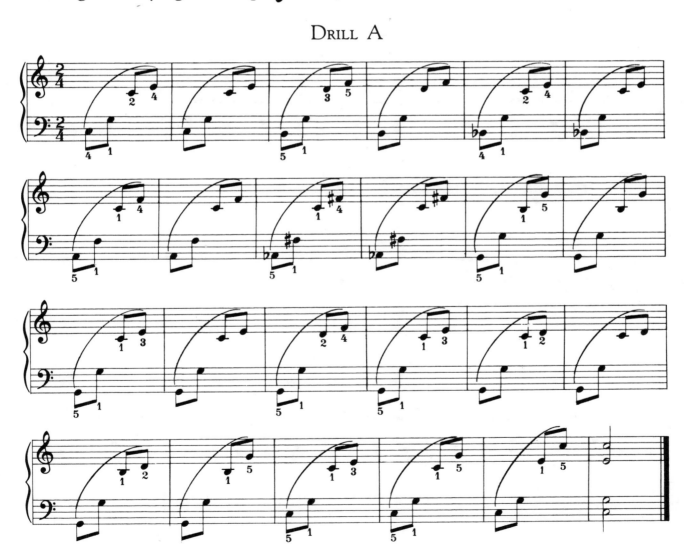

"Three To Get Ready"

IN DRILL B you will work to achieve greater control over the third, fourth and fifth fingers of your right hand, both in legato and staccato.

First Reading
Right hand alone. Play *mf* (mezzo forte — moderately loud). ♪=120-144.

Second Reading
Right hand alone. Play *mf.* ♪=160-184.

Third Reading
Right hand alone. Play *mf.* ♩=80-92.

Fourth Reading
Left hand alone. Play *p* (piano — soft). ♩=80-92.

Fifth Reading
Hands together. Play *mf* in the right hand and *p* in the left hand. ♩=80-92.

Sixth Reading
Hands together. Play *mf* in the right hand and *p* in the left hand. ♩=108-120.

DRILL B

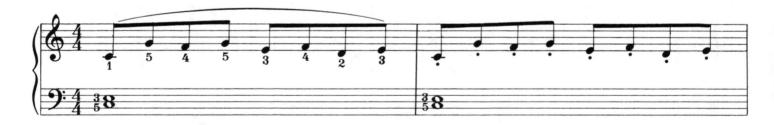

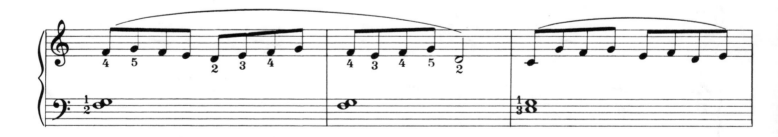

"The Long And Short Of It"

DRILL C concentrates on improving control of the third, fourth and fifth fingers of your left hand. In addition, the practice technique used in the Fourth and Fifth Readings of Drill C can be used in other drills, and in many pieces.

First Reading
Left hand alone. Play legato (smooth and connected) and *mf* (mezzo forte—moderately loud). ♪=120-138.

Second Reading
Left hand alone. Play legato and *mf.* ♪=144-184.

Third Reading
Left hand alone. Play legato and *mf.* ♩=72-92.

Fourth Reading
Left hand alone. Play legato and *mf.* A good way to improve your control over any passage which is written in a continuous rhythm is to practice it in different rhythmic patterns of long and short note values. This "trick" can easily be applied to the left hand of Drill C. In the example shown below the rhythmic values of the notes of the left hand are changed to a pattern of long and short. Each measure is equal to one measure of the original drill. Play the entire drill using this pattern. ♩=72-92.

Fifth Reading
Left hand alone. Play legato and *mf.* Reverse the rhythmic pattern used in the Fourth Reading. In this case the rhythmic values are changed to short and long. Play the entire drill using the rhythmic variation shown below. ♩=72-92.

Sixth Reading
Right hand alone. Play legato and *mp* (mezzo piano—moderately soft). ♩=72-92.

Seventh Reading
Hands together as written. Play the left hand *mf* and the right hand *mp.* ♩=72-92.

Eighth Reading
Hands together. Play the left hand *mf* and the right hand *mp.* ♩=104-120.

(Drill on next page)

DRILL C

Etude No. 49

CARL CZERNY

WEEK
4

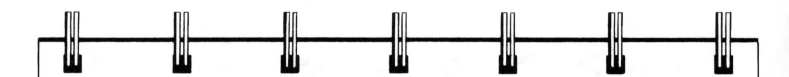

Monday	Drill A, First Reading, 5 Minutes Drill B, First Reading, 5 Minutes Drill C, First Reading, 5 Minutes Drill C, Second Reading, 5 Minutes
Tuesday	Drill C, Second Reading, 5 Minutes Drill B, First Reading, 5 Minutes Drill B, Second Reading, 5 Minutes Drill A, Second Reading, 5 Minutes
Wednesday	Drill C, Third Reading, 5 Minutes Drill C, Fourth Reading, 5 Minutes Drill A, Third Reading, 5 Minutes Drill B, Third Reading, 5 Minutes
Thursday	Drill C, Fourth Reading, 5 Minutes Drill A, Fifth Reading, 5 Minutes Drill A, Fifth Reading, 5 Minutes Drill B, Fourth Reading, 5 Minutes
Friday	Drill B, Fourth Reading, 5 Minutes Drill B, Fifth Reading, 5 Minutes Drill C, Fifth Reading, 5 Minutes Drill A, Sixth Reading, 5 Minutes
Sat/Sun	Drill B, Fifth Reading, 5 Minutes Drill B, Sixth Reading, 5 Minutes Drill A, Sixth Reading, 5 Minutes Drill C, Fifth Reading, 5 Minutes

"Thumbs Up"

DESIGNED to help you develop independence between the fourth and fifth fingers, Drill A also requires you to place your thumb on both black and white keys. Remember that when you play a black key with the thumb or the fifth finger it is necessary to move the hand in closer to the lid of the piano.

First Reading
Right hand alone. Play legato (smooth and connected) and *mf* (mezzo forte—moderately loud). ♪=116-138.

Second Reading
Right hand alone. Play legato and *mf.* ♪ =144-184.

Third Reading
Right hand alone. Play legato and *p* (piano — soft). ♩=72-92.

Fourth Reading
Left hand alone. Play *p* and legato. ♩=72-92.

Fifth Reading
Hands together. Play the right hand *mf* and the left hand *p.* ♩=72-92.

Sixth Reading
Hands together. Play the right hand *mf* and the left hand *p.* ♩=104-120.

DRILL A

DRILL B is unusual because it does not use the thumb in either hand. Notice that the four-note groups (which are groups of four fingers) are written under one slur. Make a "break" (or detach) between the slurs. The two hands are played one octave apart throughout.

First Reading

Left hand alone. Play legato (smooth and connected) and *p* (piano — soft). ♪=126-152.

Second Reading

Right hand alone. Play legato and *p*. ♪=126-152.

Third Reading

Hands together. Play legato and *p*. ♪=126-152.

Fourth Reading

Hands together. Play legato and *p*. ♩=72-80.

Fifth Reading

Hands together. Move each hand up one octave (8 keys) throughout the entire piece. Play staccato (short and separated) and *mf* (mezzo forte — moderately loud). ♩=88-104.

Sixth Reading

Hands together. Play as written. Play legato and *f* (forte — loud). ♩=116-132.

DRILL B

"Czern-ing It Out"

CARL CZERNY (pronounced Chair-knee) was one of the most influential pianists of his time. A student of Beethoven and the teacher of Liszt, he occupies an important place in the transition between the Classical Period and the Romantic Period. He is best known for the hundreds of Etudes (Studies) he composed. One of the best features of Czerny's Etudes is that while they were composed as studies to help improve technique, they are really pieces of music which are enjoyable to play. When playing this Etude be sure to listen for the melody, whether it is played by the right or left hand; be careful not to let the chords of the accompaniment cover it up.

First Reading
Right hand alone. Play legato (smooth and connected) and *mf* (mezzo forte—moderately loud). ♩=72-80.

Second Reading
Right hand alone. Play legato and *mf*. ♩=88-92.

Third Reading
Left hand alone. Play *p* (piano—soft). Be certain to use the fingering indicated. ♩=72-80.

Fourth Reading
Hands together. Play the right hand *mf* and the left hand *p*. ♩=72-80.

Fifth Reading
Hands together. Play the right hand *mf* and the left hand *p*. ♩=92-120.

(Drill on next page)

Drill C

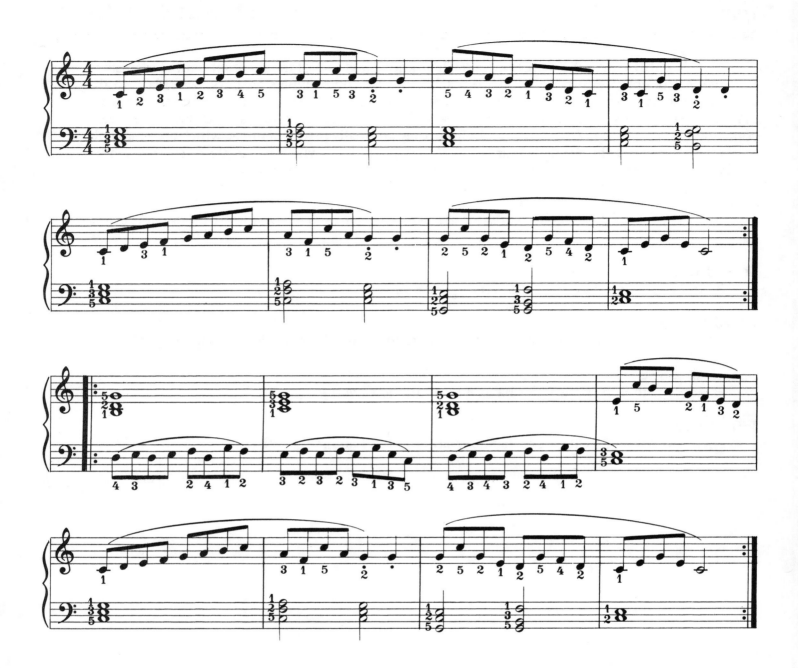

An Old Legend

Opus 107

CARL REINECKE

Molto tranquillo

WEEK
5

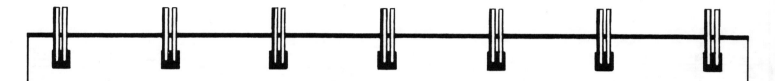

Monday	Drill A, First Reading, 5 Minutes Drill A, Second Reading, 5 Minutes Drill B, First Reading, 5 Minutes Drill B, Second Reading, 5 Minutes
Tuesday	Drill C, First Reading, 5 Minutes Drill C, Second Reading, 5 Minutes Drill B, Second Reading, 5 Minutes Drill A, Second Reading, 5 Minutes
Wednesday	Drill A, Third Reading, 5 Minutes Drill A, Fourth Reading, 5 Minutes Drill C, First and Second Readings, 5 Minutes Drill C, Third Reading, 5 Minutes
Thursday	Drill C, Third Reading, 5 Minutes Drill B, Third Reading, 5 Minutes Drill A, Fourth Reading, 5 Minutes Drill A, Fifth Reading, 5 Minutes
Friday	Drill C, Fourth Reading, 5 Minutes Drill C, Fifth Reading, 5 Minutes Drill B, Fourth Reading, 5 Minutes Drill A, Sixth Reading, 5 Minutes
Sat/Sun	Drill B, Fifth Reading, 5 Minutes Drill A, Seventh Reading, 5 Minutes Drill C, Fourth Reading, 5 Minutes Drill C, Fifth Reading, 5 Minutes

"Running In Place"

REPEATED notes may be played in two ways: 1. by playing each successive note with a different finger, or 2. by using the same finger on each note and repeating the note by playing with a hand and wrist action. Both methods have their merits, and either one or both may work for you. By playing Drill A using each of these methods of fingering, you can find the one that is best for you.

First Reading

Hands together. Play staccato (short and separated) and *mp* (mezzo piano—moderately soft). Change fingers on each of the repeated notes. ♪=96-116.

Second Reading

Hands together. Play staccato and *mp*. Change fingers on each of the repeated notes. ♪=120-152.

Third Reading

Hands together. Play staccato and *mp*. Change fingers on each of the repeated notes. ♩=60-80.

Fourth Reading

Hands together. Play staccato and *mp*. Play all of the repeated notes with your thumb. ♪=96-116.

Fifth Reading

Hands together. Play staccato and *mp*. Play all of the repeated notes with your thumb. ♪=120-152.

Sixth Reading

Hands together. Play staccato and *mp*. Play all of the repeated notes with your thumb. ♩=60-80.

Seventh Reading

Hands together. Play staccato and *mp*. Select the fingering you think is best for you. ♩=92-116.

(Drill on next page)

Drill A

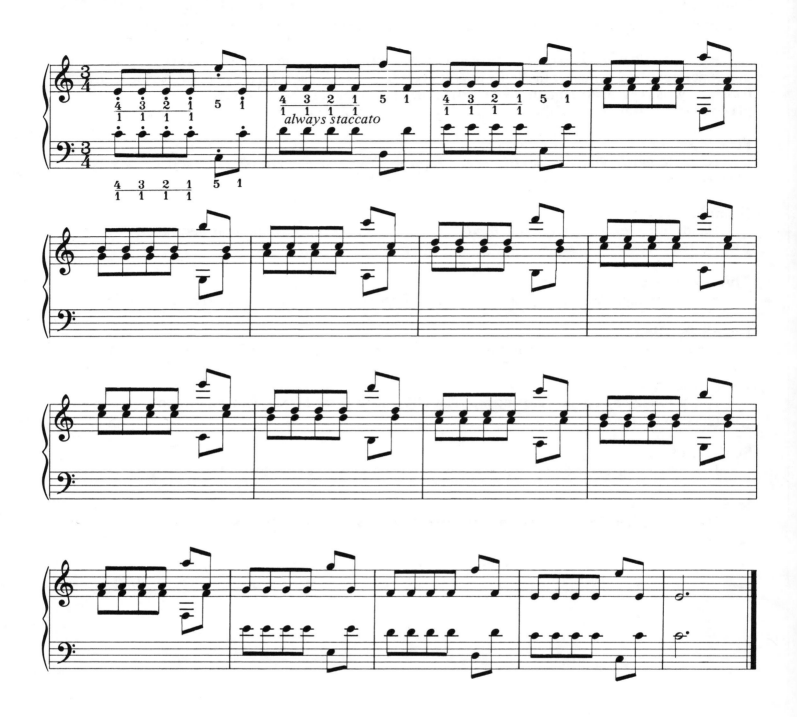

"Left Alone Again"

DRILL B gives you a good opportunity to develop the third, fourth and fifth fingers of your left hand.

First Reading
Left hand alone. Play legato (smooth and connected) and *mf* (mezzo forte—moderately loud). ♩=96-116.

Second Reading
Left hand alone. Play legato and *p* (piano — soft). ♩=120-138.

Third Reading
Left hand alone. Play staccato (short and separated) and *p.* ♩=144-160.

Fourth Reading
Left hand alone. Play staccato and *mf.* Move your hand up one octave. ♩=168-176.

Fifth Reading
Left hand alone. Play legato and *f* (forte — loud). Play as written. ♩=176-184.

DRILL B

"Follow The Berti"

CZERNY uses one of the Eighteenth Century's (the Classical Period) most popular devices in this etude—the "Alberti" bass. This broken chord figure found in the left hand of Drill C is named after Domenico Alberti (1710-1740), who used this figuration in his 36 Sonatas. Although he probably did not actually invent it, Alberti's name is permanently linked to this type of accompaniment figure.

First Reading
Left hand alone. Play legato (smooth and connected) and **p** (piano — soft). ♩=72-84.

Second Reading
Right hand alone. Play legato and **mf** (mezzo forte — moderately loud). ♩=72-84.

Third Reading
Hands together. Play legato. Play the right hand **mf** and the left hand **p**. ♩=72-84.

Fourth Reading
Hands together. Play legato. Play the right hand **mf** and the left hand **p**. ♩=92-116.

Fifth Reading
Hands together. Play legato. Play the right hand **mf** and the left hand **p**. ♩=120-132.

Drill C

Etude No. 1

FRIEDRICH WEICK

WEEK
6

Monday	Drill A, First Reading, 5 Minutes Drill A, Second Reading, 5 Minutes Drill B, First Reading, 5 Minutes Drill B, Second Reading, 5 Minutes
Tuesday	Drill B, Third Reading, 5 Minutes Drill C, First Reading, 5 Minutes Drill C, Second Reading, 5 Minutes Drill A, Second Reading, 5 Minutes
Wednesday	Drill A, Second Reading, 5 Minutes Drill A, Third Reading, 5 Minutes Drill C, Third Reading, 10 Minutes
Thursday	Drill B, Fourth Reading, 5 Minutes Drill A, Fourth Reading, 5 Minutes Drill C, Fourth Reading, 5 Minutes Drill C, Fifth Reading, 5 Minutes
Friday	Drill A, Fifth Reading, 5 Minutes Drill A, Sixth Reading, 5 Minutes Drill B, Fifth Reading, 5 Minutes Drill C, Sixth Reading, 5 Minutes
Sat/Sun	Drill C, Sixth Reading, 5 Minutes Drill B, Fifth Reading, 5 Minutes Drill A, Seventh Reading, 10 Minutes

"Up and Down"

THIS beneficial exercise uses interesting chords to help further develop your control over the fourth and fifth fingers.

First Reading
Right hand alone. Play legato (smooth and connected) and *mf* (mezzo forte—moderately loud). ♪=120-144.

Second Reading
Left hand alone. Play legato and *mf.* ♪=120-144.

Third Reading
Hands together. Play legato and *mf.* ♩=60-72.

Fourth Reading
Hands together. Play legato and *mf.* Using the same practice "trick" learned in Week 3, practice Drill A with the following variation of long and short rhythmic values. ♩=72-80.

Fifth Reading
Hands together. Play legato and *mf.* Reverse the rhythmic variation used in the Fourth Reading. ♩=72-80.

Sixth Reading
Hands together. Move the right hand up one octave and move the left hand down one octave. Play legato and *p* (piano — soft). ♩=92-108.

Seventh Reading
Hands together, as written. Play legato and *f* (forte — loud). ♩=112-126.

Drill A

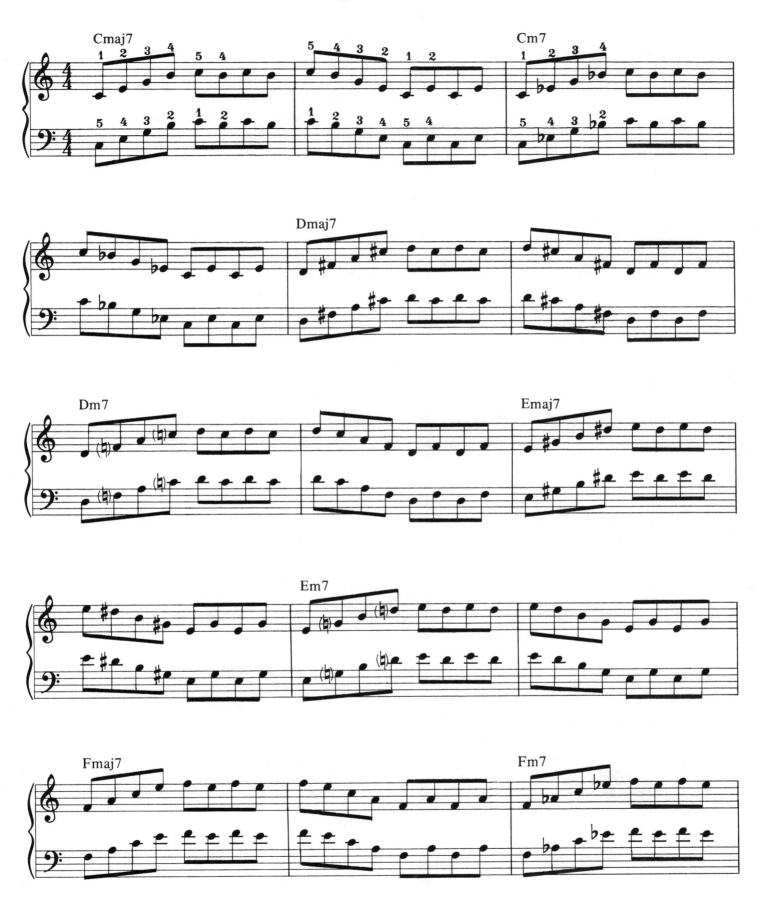

(continued on next page)

41

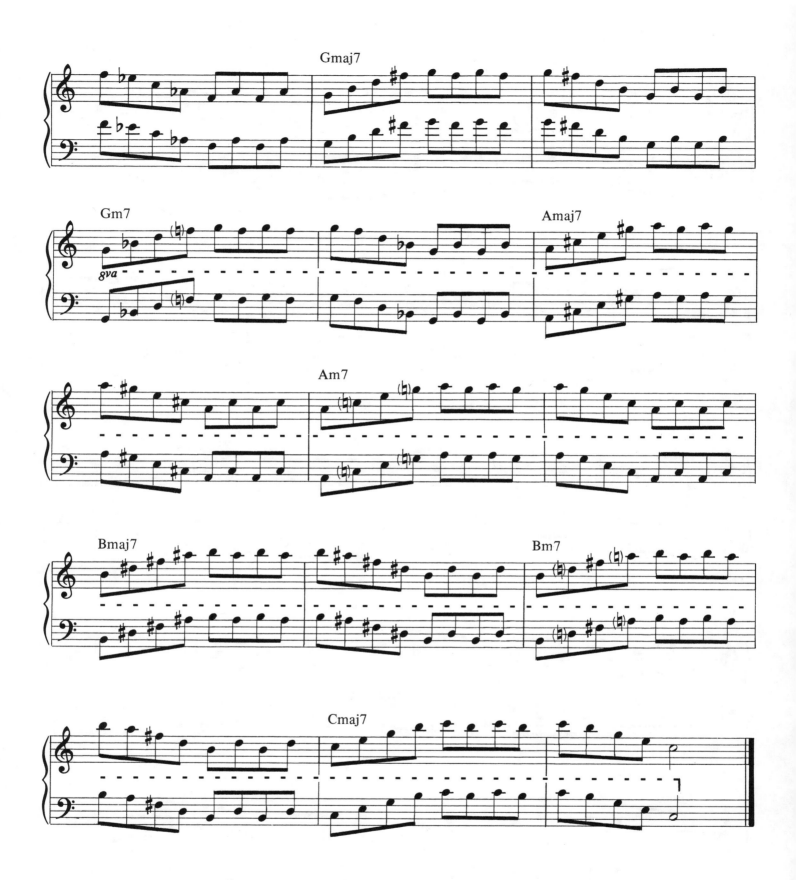

"Broken Up"

DRILL B is a study in broken chords within the space of one octave. The accents marked in the score will help you achieve clarity. Let your wrist and arm follow the fingers. Do not cause your arm to stay in one place, forcing your fingers to stretch in order to find the notes. Instead, feel free to let the wrist and arm move so you can reach the notes easily.

First Reading

Right hand alone. Observe the slurs and staccato dots carefully. Play *mp* (mezzo piano — moderately loud). Remember that the triplets ( ) are slightly faster than the eighth notes ( ). ♩=72-88.

Second Reading

Left hand alone. Observe the slurs and staccato dots carefully. Play *mp.* Try to make the left hand sound exactly like the right hand. ♩=72-88.

Third Reading

Hands together. Play *f* (forte — loud). ♩=92-108.

Fourth Reading

Hands together. Play *p* (piano — soft). Move the hands up one octave. ♩=112-120.

Fifth Reading

Hands together. Play as written. Play *mf.* ♩=126-138.

(Drill on next page)

44

DO NOT BE frightened by the black ink of the sixteenth notes. They do not necessarily go at a quick tempo. Four sixteenth notes equals one quarter note (♬♬ = ♩). For practice you may sub-divide the beat into two parts, in which case two sixteenth notes equal one eighth note (♬ = ♪).

Week 4, Drill B was based on a four-note pattern that did not use the thumb. This Drill is also written on a four-note pattern, but uses the thumb. In this case, the four-note groups are connected and are to be played legato.

First Reading
  Right hand alone. Play legato (smooth and connected) and *p* (piano — soft). ♪=92-108.

Second Reading
  Left hand alone. Play legato and *p.* ♪=92-108.

Third Reading
  Hands together. Play legato and *p.* ♪=92-108.

Fourth Reading
  Hands together. Play staccato (short and separated) and *f* (forte — loud). ♪=112-132.

Fifth Reading
  Hands together. Play legato and *f.* ♩=60-72.

Sixth Reading
  Hands together. Play legato and *mf* (mezzo forte — moderately loud). ♩=80-92.

DRILL C

Study No. 1

J. B CRAMER

Allegro

WEEK
7

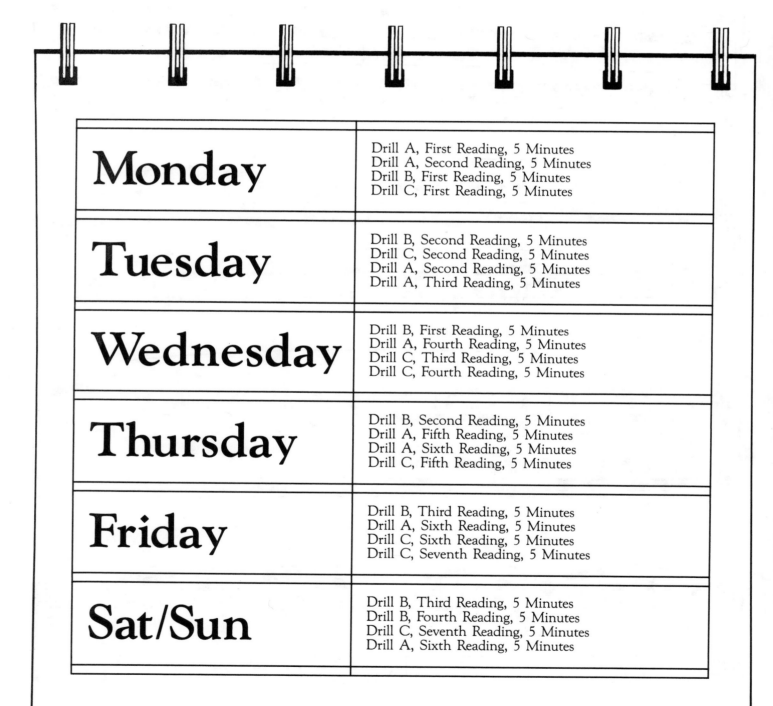

Monday	Drill A, First Reading, 5 Minutes Drill A, Second Reading, 5 Minutes Drill B, First Reading, 5 Minutes Drill C, First Reading, 5 Minutes
Tuesday	Drill B, Second Reading, 5 Minutes Drill C, Second Reading, 5 Minutes Drill A, Second Reading, 5 Minutes Drill A, Third Reading, 5 Minutes
Wednesday	Drill B, First Reading, 5 Minutes Drill A, Fourth Reading, 5 Minutes Drill C, Third Reading, 5 Minutes Drill C, Fourth Reading, 5 Minutes
Thursday	Drill B, Second Reading, 5 Minutes Drill A, Fifth Reading, 5 Minutes Drill A, Sixth Reading, 5 Minutes Drill C, Fifth Reading, 5 Minutes
Friday	Drill B, Third Reading, 5 Minutes Drill A, Sixth Reading, 5 Minutes Drill C, Sixth Reading, 5 Minutes Drill C, Seventh Reading, 5 Minutes
Sat/Sun	Drill B, Third Reading, 5 Minutes Drill B, Fourth Reading, 5 Minutes Drill C, Seventh Reading, 5 Minutes Drill A, Sixth Reading, 5 Minutes

"Finger Oil"

MOST of the difficulty of this Drill lies in the right hand. Do not let the left hand, with its rather thick chords, overpower the right hand, which is the "melody."

First Reading
Right hand alone. Play legato and *mf.* ♪=104-116.

Second Reading
Right hand alone. Play legato and *mf.* ♪=120-132 (♩=60-66).

Third Reading
Left hand alone. Play *mf* as legato as possible. ♩=66-72.

Fourth Reading
Hands together. Play legato and *mf.* ♩=60-66.

Fifth Reading
Hands together. Play legato and *mf.* ♩=72-84.

Sixth Reading
Hands together. Play legato and *mf.* ♩=92-108.

(Drill on next page)

Drill A

I**T WOULD** be difficult to find a more beneficial study than this one for achieving control over the fingers (finger independence). Although this drill is quite difficult to play with complete control, its value in helping you improve your technique makes it well worth the effort. Remember that you are practicing to achieve finger independence. Keep in mind that your goal is not to be able to play this exercise with ease right away, but instead to work in that direction.

The notes in parenthesis are to be held silently at the surface of the keys WITHOUT DEPRESSING THEM IN THE LEAST!

First Reading
Right hand alone. Play **p.** =92-108.

Second Reading
Left hand alone. Play **p.** =92-108.

Third Reading
Right hand alone. Play *f.* =92-108.

Fourth Reading
Left hand alone. Play *f.* =92-108.

DRILL B

"Musical Tendon-cies"

BECAUSE our third and fourth fingers are connected by a tendon, it is unusually difficult to achieve control of these fingers. This exercise focuses on this problem. Remember that speed is not the most important aspect of this or any etude. Work to achieve control.

First Reading
Right hand alone. Play *mp* and legato. ♪=92-104.

Second Reading
Right hand alone. Play legato and *mf*. ♪=112-132.

Third Reading
Right hand alone. Play legato and *mf*. Use the following rhythmic variation: ♩=72-80.

Fourth Reading
Left hand alone. Play *p*. ♩=66-80.

Fifth Reading
Hands together. Play the right hand *mf* and the left hand *p*. ♪=92-104.

Sixth Reading
Hands together. Play the right hand *mf* and the left hand *p*. ♪=120-144 (♩=60-72).

Seventh Reading
Hands together. Play the right hand *mf* and the left hand *p*. ♩=80-96.

DRILL C

Gypsy Dance

JOSEF HAYDN

Allegro

WEEK
8

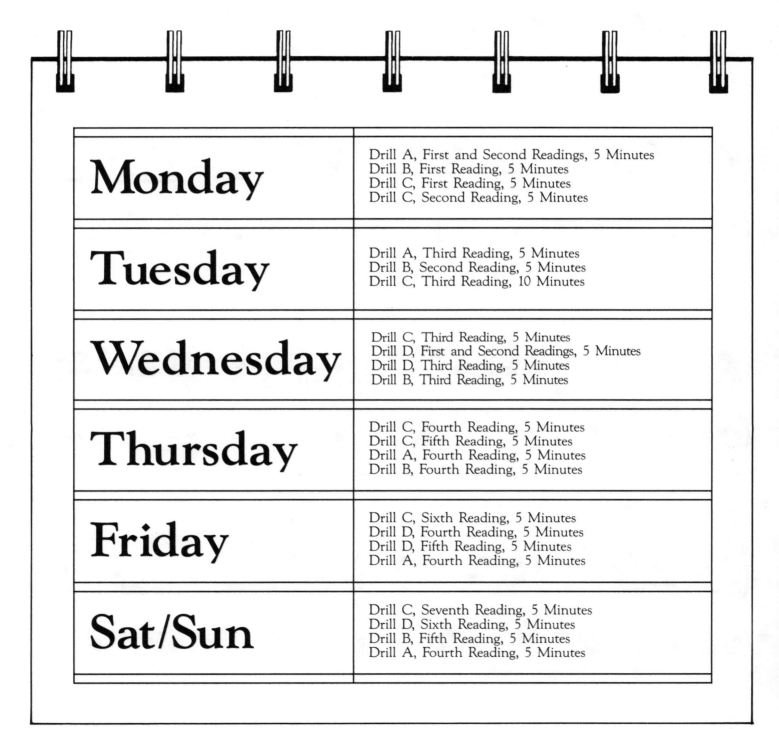

Monday	Drill A, First and Second Readings, 5 Minutes Drill B, First Reading, 5 Minutes Drill C, First Reading, 5 Minutes Drill C, Second Reading, 5 Minutes
Tuesday	Drill A, Third Reading, 5 Minutes Drill B, Second Reading, 5 Minutes Drill C, Third Reading, 10 Minutes
Wednesday	Drill C, Third Reading, 5 Minutes Drill D, First and Second Readings, 5 Minutes Drill D, Third Reading, 5 Minutes Drill B, Third Reading, 5 Minutes
Thursday	Drill C, Fourth Reading, 5 Minutes Drill C, Fifth Reading, 5 Minutes Drill A, Fourth Reading, 5 Minutes Drill B, Fourth Reading, 5 Minutes
Friday	Drill C, Sixth Reading, 5 Minutes Drill D, Fourth Reading, 5 Minutes Drill D, Fifth Reading, 5 Minutes Drill A, Fourth Reading, 5 Minutes
Sat/Sun	Drill C, Seventh Reading, 5 Minutes Drill D, Sixth Reading, 5 Minutes Drill B, Fifth Reading, 5 Minutes Drill A, Fourth Reading, 5 Minutes

"Side-Stepping"

DRILL A is written to help you develop freedom in lateral (side-wise) movements of the hand. Do not hold your elbow too close to your body as you play. Feel free to move your arm and hand as much as necessary in order to reach the notes.

First Reading

Right hand alone. Play legato and *mf.* ♪=120-144 (♩=60-72).

Second Reading

Left hand alone. Play legato and *mf.* ♪=120-144 (♩=60-72).

Third Reading

Hands together. Play legato and *mf.* ♩=72-84.

Fourth Reading

Hands together. Play legato and *mf.* ♩=88-96.

DRILL A

"Skip And Step"

Extensions and contractions—that is, notes which are close together followed by notes which are separated by a distance—can be a difficult aspect of piano technique. This drill concentrates again on the left hand, with attention to this particular kind of playing situation.

First Reading
Left hand alone. Play legato and *p.* ♪=104-120.

Second Reading
Left hand alone. Play legato and *f.* ♩=60-72.

Third Reading
Left hand alone. Play staccato and *p.* ♩=76-88.

Fourth Reading
Left hand alone. Play staccato and *f.* ♩=92-104.

Fifth Reading
Left hand alone. Play legato and *mp.* ♩=120-144.

Drill B

"Waltzing"

THIS DRILL is composed of two clearly distinct parts—a melody and an accompaniment. The accompaniment consists of a series of broken chords. The tempo indication—Vivace—means lively. That does not necessarily mean fast.

First Reading

Left hand alone. In measures 1-16, play the accompaniment figure (broken chords) as blocked chords, playing all three notes of each beat as a chord.

When the left hand begins to play the melody in measure 17, play as written, but in measure 25 switch back to blocked chords. ♩=72-96.

Second Reading

Right hand alone. Measures 1-16, play as written. Measures 17-24, play the three notes of each beat together as a chord. ♩=72-96.

Third Reading

Hands together. Play the left hand as chords in measures 1-16 and measures 25-32. In measures 17-24 play the right hand as chords. ♩=72-96.

Fourth Reading

Left hand alone as written. Play legato and **p.** ♩=72-96.

Fifth Reading

Right hand alone as written. Observe the slurs and staccato dots. ♩=72-96.

Sixth Reading

Hands together as written. ♩=72-96.

Seventh Reading

Hands together. ♩=112-120.

(Drill on next page)

Drill C

"Hands In Tandem"

THE lateral (side-wise) movements of the hand you worked on in Drill A will help you play Drill D.

First Reading
Left hand alone. Play *mp* and legato. ♪=100-112.

Second Reading
Right hand alone. Play *mp* and legato. ♪=100-112.

Third Reading
Hands together. Play legato and *mp.* ♪=100-112.

Fourth Reading
Hands together. Play staccato and *mp.* ♪=100-112.

Fifth Reading
Hands together. Play legato and *mp.* ♪=126-152.

Sixth Reading
Hands together. Play legato and *mp.* ♪=144-184 (♩=72-92).

DRILL D

Sonatina

Opus 36, No. 2

Muzio Clementi

WEEK
9

Monday	Drill A, First Reading, 5 Minutes Drill B, First Reading, 5 Minutes Drill C, First Reading, 5 Minutes Drill C, Second Reading, 5 Minutes
Tuesday	Drill A, Second Reading, 5 Minutes Drill C, First and Second Readings, 5 Minutes Drill C, Third Reading, 5 Minutes Drill B, Second Reading, 5 Minutes
Wednesday	Drill C, Third Reading, 5 Minutes Drill A, Third Reading, 10 Minutes Drill B, Third Reading, 5 Minutes
Thursday	Drill C, Fourth Reading, 10 Minutes Drill A, Fourth Reading, 5 Minutes Drill B, Fourth Reading, 5 Minutes
Friday	Drill B, Fourth Reading, 5 Minutes Drill A, Fifth Reading, 5 Minutes Drill C, Fifth Reading, 5 Minutes Drill C, Sixth Reading, 5 Minutes
Sat/Sun	Drill C, Sixth Reading, 5 Minutes Drill B, Fourth Reading, 5 Minutes Drill A, Fifth Reading, 5 Minutes Drill C, Sixth Reading, 5 Minutes

"Hands Together"

DURING Week 3 we worked on connecting notes between the hands (Drill A). This Drill is a more complex version of that musical situation. Remember to be especially careful when connecting the thumbs. Try to imagine how each two-beat group would sound if it were played by one hand. Aim to make certain that there is no difference in tone quality between the hands.

First Reading
Hands together. Play legato and *mp.* ♪=84-100.

Second Reading
Hands together. Play legato and *mp.* ♪=108-126.

Third Reading
Hands together. Play staccato and *p.* ♪=138-160 (♩=64-80).

Fourth Reading
Hands together. Play legato and *f.* ♩=80-92.

Fifth Reading
Hands together. Play legato and *mp.* ♩=96-108.

(Drill on next page)

Drill A

64

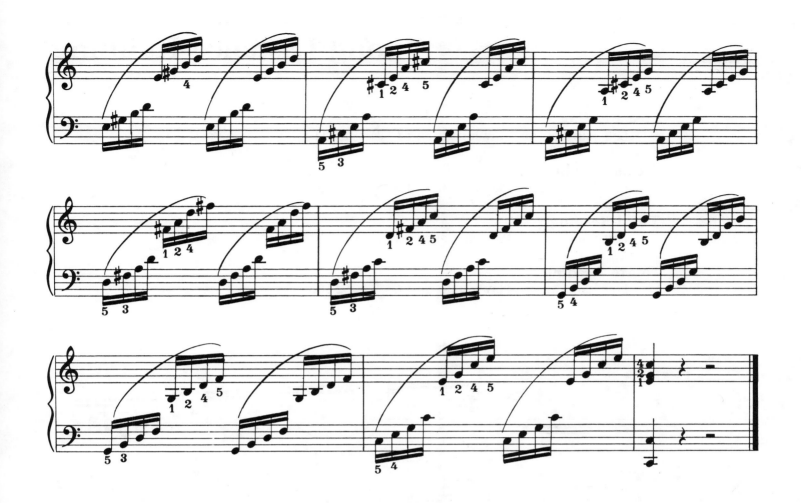

"Long Distance Running"

First Reading
Left hand alone. Play legato and *f.* ♪=92-104.

Second Reading
Left hand alone. Play legato and *p.* ♪=116-132.

Third Reading
Left hand alone. Play staccato and *p.* ♪=132-144.

Fourth Reading
Left hand alone. Play legato and *f.* ♪=152-168.

Drill B

"Taking Turns"

Kohler combines five-finger patterns and scales in the following study. Throughout there is a continuous sixteenth-note rhythm, although it shifts between the right hand and the left hand. Be certain that the tempo does not change when the sixteenth notes shift from the right hand to the left.

First Reading

Right hand alone. Play legato and observe the dynamics in the score. ♪=92-104.

Second Reading

Left hand alone. Play legato and observe the dynamics in the score. ♪=92-104.

Third Reading

Hands together. Play legato. ♪=72-92.

Fourth Reading

Hands together. Increase the tempo to ♪=104-120 (♩=52-60).

Fifth Reading

Hands together. ♩=66-80.

Sixth Reading

Hands together. ♩=84-104.

(Drill on next page)

Drill C

Etude

HENRY BERTINI

WEEK 10

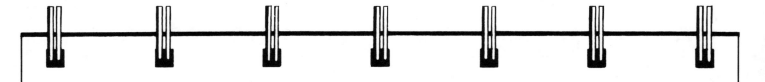

Monday	Drill A, First Reading, 5 Minutes Drill B, First Reading, 5 Minutes Drill B, Second Reading, 5 Minutes Drill C, First Reading, 5 Minutes
Tuesday	Drill C, First Reading, 5 Minutes Drill C, Second Reading, 5 Minutes Drill A, Second Reading, 5 Minutes Drill B, Third Reading, 5 Minutes
Wednesday	Drill A, First Reading, 5 Minutes Drill B, Third Reading, 5 Minutes Drill B, Fourth Reading, 5 Minutes Drill C, Third Reading, 5 Minutes
Thursday	Drill C, Third Reading, 5 Minutes Drill C, Fourth Reading, 5 Minutes Drill B, Fifth Reading, 10 Minutes
Friday	Drill A, Second Reading, 5 Minutes Drill C, Fifth Reading, 5 Minutes Drill B, Sixth Reading, 10 Minutes
Sat/Sun	Drill B, Sixth Reading, 5 Minutes Drill A, First and Second Readings, 5 Minutes Drill C, Fifth Reading, 5 Minutes Drill C, Sixth Reading, 5 Minutes

THIS exercise is a variation of Drill B, Week 7. When you were practicing that exercise you no doubt found that the most difficult aspect is to avoid depressing the keys on which you are resting your fingers. Keeping them at the surface level is not a question of holding your fingers up, but of NOT using unnecessary muscles. Always keep in mind that you are working toward your goal of greater finger independence.

First Reading

Right hand alone. Observe the dynamics indicated in the score. ♩=72-80.

Second Reading

Left hand alone. Observe the dynamics indicated in the score. ♩=72-80.

DRILL A

"Perpetual Motion"

THIS etude makes us cross over the thumb, and in addition has extensions between the third and fifth fingers and between the second and fourth. At a fast tempo it is fairly hard to control.

First Reading

Right hand alone. Play *f* and legato. ♪=112-120.

Second Reading

Left hand alone. Play staccato as marked and legato in measures 9-14. ♪=112-120.

Third Reading

Right hand alone, measures 1-8 only. In previous chapters we have seen how practicing technically difficult passages written in a continuous rhythmic pattern can benefit by the addition of rhythmic variation. Try practicing by holding the first note of each group of four sixteenth notes longer than normal. Next, play the other notes of the group as quickly as possible.

After you have practiced measures 1-8 following the pattern shown above, elongate first the second note of each group of four, then the third note, and finally the fourth note.

Fourth Reading

Left hand alone, measures 9-12 only. Play these measures using the rhythmic variations described above.

Fifth Reading

Hands together as written. ♪=132-144 (♩=66-72).

Sixth Reading

Hands together. Increase the tempo to ♩=88-100.

Drill B

"Rock And Roll"

IT IS probably obvious to you that the following etude needs to be practiced hands separately at first, since each hand plays an independent part.

First Reading

Right hand alone. Play legato and *p* and *f* as marked in the music. ♩=72-80.

Second Reading

Left hand alone. Play legato and staccato as marked. Be sure to make a difference between the slurs (legato) and staccato. Play *p* and *f* as indicated. ♩=72-80.

Third Reading

Right hand alone. ♩=92-108.

Fourth Reading

Left hand alone. ♩=92-108.

Fifth Reading

Hands together. ♩=72-80.

Sixth Reading

Hands together. Increase tempo to ♩=92-108.

Drill C

Etude No. 45

Allegro vivace

CARL CZERNY

D. C. al Fine

WEEK
11

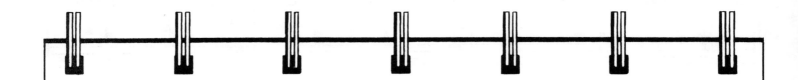

Monday	Drill A, First Reading, 10 Minutes Drill B, First Reading, 5 Minutes Drill C, First Reading, 5 Minutes
Tuesday	Drill C, First Reading, 5 Minutes Drill C, Second Reading, 5 Minutes Drill B, Second Reading, 5 Minutes Drill B, Third Reading, 5 Minutes
Wednesday	Drill A, Second Reading, 5 Minutes Drill C, Third Reading, 5 Minutes Drill B, Second Reading, 5 Minutes Drill B, Third Reading, 5 Minutes
Thursday	Drill A, Third Reading, 5 Minutes Drill A, Fourth Reading, 5 Minutes Drill B, Fourth Reading, 5 Minutes Drill C, Fourth Reading, 5 Minutes
Friday	Drill A, Fourth Reading, 5 Minutes Drill B, Fifth Reading, 5 Minutes Drill C, Fifth Reading, 5 Minutes Drill C, Sixth Reading, 5 Minutes
Sat/Sun	Drill A, Fourth Reading, 10 Minutes Drill B, Sixth Reading, 5 Minutes Drill C, Sixth Reading, 5 Minutes

"Hand to Hand"

THROUGHOUT this study the music is passed back and forth between the hands. There should be no "breaks" in the sound or rhythm. Make sure that you do not pause as you shift from the left hand to the right. Practice hands together from the outset.

First Reading

Hands together. Play legato. Observe the dynamic markings. ♪=80-96.

Second Reading

Hands together. Play legato. Observe the dynamic markings. ♪=104-120.

Third Reading

Hands together. Play legato. Observe the dynamic markings. ♪=120-138 (♩=60-69).

Fourth Reading

Hands together. Play legato. Observe the dynamic markings. ♩=72-96.

(Drill on next page)

DRILL A

"The Harp"

WHEN playing black key octaves in either the right hand or the left hand, it is often convenient to use the fourth finger in place of the fifth. (See measures 2 and 6.)

First Reading

Right hand alone. Play legato and *mf.* Follow the fingering carefully. As you play, tap the first beat of each measure with your left hand. ♪=132-160.

Second Reading

Right hand alone. Play legato and *mf.* Tap the first beat of each measure with your left hand. Use the following rhythmic variation:
♪=72-80.

Third Reading

Right hand alone. Tap the first beat of each measure with your left hand. Play legato and *mf.* Use the following rhythmic variation:
♪=72-80.

Fourth Reading

Left hand alone. ♩=72-80.

Fifth Reading

Hands together. Play as written. ♪=144-160 (♩=72-80).

Sixth Reading

Hands together. Increase the tempo to ♩=84-88.

DRILL B

"Black And White"

CZERNY combines chromatic (half-step) scale figures and diatonic (white key) scale figures in this study. Beginning in measure 4, notice the finger groups of 4 fingers (4 3 2 1) which repeat the same pattern to the end.

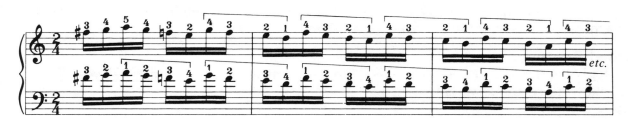

First Reading
Right hand alone. Play legato and *mp.* ♪=104-120.

Second Reading
Left hand alone. Play legato and *mp.* ♪=104-120.

Third Reading
Hands together. Play legato and *mp.* ♪=104-120.

Fourth Reading
Hands together. Play staccato and *mf.* ♪=120-144 (♩=60-72).

Fifth Reading
Hands together. Play legato and *mf.* ♩=80-88.

Sixth Reading
Hands together. Move both hands up one octave. Play legato and *p.* ♩=92-100.

DRILL C

Etude No. 4

CARL CZERNY

(continued on next page)

WEEK
12

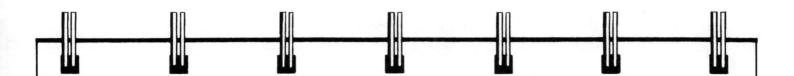

Monday	Drill A, First Reading, 5 Minutes Drill A, Second Reading, 10 Minutes Drill B, First and Second Readings, 5 Minutes
Tuesday	Drill A, Third Reading, 5 Minutes Drill A, Fourth Reading, 5 Minutes Drill B, Third Reading, 5 Minutes Drill C, First Reading, 5 Minutes
Wednesday	Drill D, First Reading, 5 Minutes Drill D, Second Reading, 5 Minutes Drill C, Second Reading, 5 Minutes Drill A, Fifth Reading, 5 Minutes
Thursday	Drill A, Sixth Reading, 5 Minutes Drill B, Fourth Reading, 5 Minutes Drill C, Third Reading, 5 Minutes Drill D, Third Reading, 5 Minutes
Friday	Drill D, Fourth Reading, 5 Minutes Drill B, Fifth Reading, 5 Minutes Drill C, Third Reading, 5 Minutes Drill A, Sixth Reading, 5 Minutes
Sat/Sun	Drill A, Fourth Reading, 5 Minutes Drill B, Fifth Reading, 5 Minutes Drill C, Third Reading, 5 Minutes Drill D, Fifth Reading, 5 Minutes

"Weaving"

ALTHOUGH Drill A is a scale study, it is really a piece of music, making it one of the most enjoyable ways to practice scales. Even at a casual glance it will be obvious that the main difficulty is placed in the right hand. When you are playing hands together, you will of necessity want to put most of your attention on the right hand. For that reason, if you know the left hand music with security you will be able to play the right hand even better. Try to memorize the left hand.

First Reading
Left hand alone. ♩=72-88.

Second Reading
Right hand alone. Play legato and **p.** ♪=100-120.

Third Reading
Right hand alone. Play legato and **p.** ♪=132-160 (♩=66-80).

Fourth Reading
Right hand alone. Play legato and **p.** Use the following rhythmic variation:

Hold the first note of each group for approximately two beats and then play the remaining three notes of the group quickly.

Fifth Reading
Right hand alone. Play legato and **p.** Use the following rhythmic variation:

Hold the third note of each group for approximately two beats and then play the following four notes quickly.

Sixth Reading
Hands together. Play as written. ♩=66-80.

Seventh Reading
Hands together. ♩=84-92.

DRILL A

"Pas De Deux"

IN DRILL B the hands play the same scale, but separated by a third. YOU MUST MEMORIZE THE FINGERING!

First Reading
    Left hand alone. Play *mf* and legato. ♪=88-112.

Second Reading
    Right hand alone. Play *mf* and legato. ♪=88-112.

Third Reading
    Hands together. Play *mf* and legato. ♪=88-112.

Fourth Reading
    Hands together. Play *mf* and legato. ♪=120-144 (♩=60-72).

Fifth Reading
    Hands together. Play *mf* and legato. ♩=76-88.

DRILL B

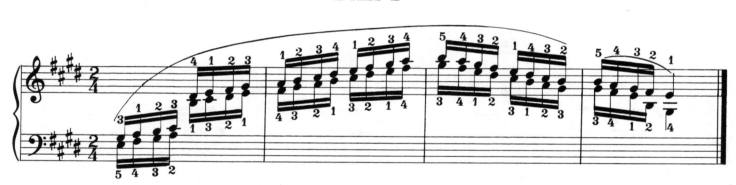

"Leaps And Bounds"

First Reading

Left hand alone. Play *f* and legato or staccato as marked. ♩=80-96.

Second Reading

Left hand alone. Play *f* and legato or staccato as marked. ♩=104-120.

Third Reading

Left hand alone. Play *f* and legato or staccato as marked. ♩=132-160.

DRILL C

"Scale Shapes"

IN DRILL D the hands are separated by the intervals of a tenth (a third plus an octave) or a sixth. It is essential that you memorize the fingering.

First Reading

Left hand alone. Play f and legato or staccato as marked. ♪=88-112.

Second Reading

Right hand alone. Play f and legato. ♪=88-112.

Third Reading

Hands together. Play f and legato or staccato as marked. ♪=88-112.

Fourth Reading

Hands together. Play f and legato or staccato as marked. ♪=120-144 (♩=60-72).

Fifth Reading

Hands together. Play f and legato or staccato as marked. ♩=76-88.

DRILL D

Etude No. 21

Opus 44

BIEHL

Week 13

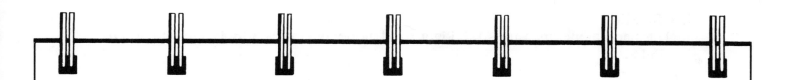

Monday	Drill A, First Reading, 5 Minutes Drill A, Second Reading, 5 Minutes Drill B, First Reading, 5 Minutes Drill C, First Reading, 5 Minutes
Tuesday	Drill A, First and Second Readings, 5 Minutes Drill A, Third Reading, 5 Minutes Drill D, First Reading, 5 Minutes Drill D, Second Reading, 5 Minutes
Wednesday	Drill A, First Reading, 5 Minutes Drills B and C, First Reading of each, 5 Minutes Drill D, Third Reading, 5 Minutes Drill D, Fourth Reading, 5 Minutes
Thursday	Drill A, Fourth Reading, 5 Minutes Drill A, Fifth Reading, 5 Minutes Drills B and C, Second Reading of each, 5 Minutes Drill D, Fifth Reading, 5 Minutes
Friday	Drill D, Fifth Reading, 5 Minutes Drill A, Fifth Reading, 5 Minutes Drill A, Sixth Reading, 5 Minutes Drills B and C, Second Reading of each, 5 Minutes
Sat/Sun	Drill A, Sixth Reading, 5 Minutes Drills B and C, Second Reading of each, 5 Minutes Drill D, Sixth Reading, 10 Minutes

Herr ("Hair") Köhler

THE ACCOMPANIMENT used by Köhler in this study is similar to the "Alberti Bass" discussed in Week 5. Although the difference is slight on paper, the figure used here is more difficult to play than the "Alberti" figure.

Alberti Bass   Measure 1

First Reading
Left hand alone, measures 1-7. Right hand alone, measures 8-16. Play legato and ***p***.
♪=116-144.

Second Reading
Left hand alone, measures 1-7. Right hand alone, measures 8-16. Play measures 1-7 (with the exception of the third and fourth beats of measure 4, which should be played as written) in blocked chords.

Play measures 8-16 in the same way (with the exception of measures 8 and 12, which should be played as written). ♩=84-96.

Third Reading
Right hand alone, measures 1-7. Left hand alone, measures 8-16. ♩=84-104.

Fourth Reading
Hands together as written. ♪=112-132.

Fifth Reading
Hands together. Increase the tempo to ♩=60-72.

Sixth Reading
Hands together. Increase the tempo to ♩=80-96.

Drill A

"Across The Keyboard"

EACH of these studies was written in order to practice arpeggios for the left hand alone. Where two fingerings are indicated for one note, you may select the finger that is most comfortable for your hand. Follow the same directions for both Drill B and Drill C. Allow your arm and wrist to move freely in order to reach the notes easily. Try to play legato, but if you cannot reach a note easily do not be afraid to "jump" to it from the previous note.

First Reading

Follow the fingering carefully. Select the finger which is best for your hand, when two fingers are indicated for one note. ♩=60.

Second Reading

Increase the tempo to ♩=66-80.

DRILL B

Drill C

"Chord-ially"

First Reading

Right hand alone, measures 1-8. Left hand alone, measures 9-16. Play legato and *f*. ♩=66-76.

Second Reading

Right hand alone, measures 1-8. Left hand alone, measures 9-16. Play all three notes of each beat together as a chord. ♩=66-76.

Third Reading

Right hand alone, measures 1-8. Left hand alone, measures 9-16. Play as written. ♩=66-76.

Fourth Reading

Left hand alone, measures 1-8. Right hand alone, measures 9-16. ♩=66-76.

Fifth Reading

Hands together as written. ♩=66-76.

Sixth Reading

Hands together. Increase the tempo to ♩=80-88.

DRILL D

Andante Cantabile

From Sonatina in F, No. 3

Antonio Diabelli

WEEK 14

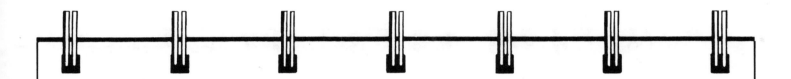

Monday	Drill A, First Reading, 5 Minutes Drill B, First Reading, 5 Minutes Drill B, Second Reading, 5 Minutes Drill C, First Reading, 5 Minutes
Tuesday	Drill C, First Reading, 5 Minutes Drill C, Second Reading, 5 Minutes Drill A, Second Reading, 5 Minutes Drill A, Third Reading, 5 Minutes
Wednesday	Drill B, Third Reading, 5 Minutes Drill B, Fourth Reading, 5 Minutes Drill C, Third Reading, 5 Minutes Drill C, Fourth Reading, 5 Minutes
Thursday	Drill A, Fourth Reading, 5 Minutes Drill B, Fifth Reading, 5 Minutes Drill C, Fourth Reading, 5 Minutes Drill C, Fifth Reading, 5 Minutes
Friday	Drill A, Fifth Reading, 5 Minutes Drill B, Sixth Reading, 5 Minutes Drill B, Seventh Reading, 5 Minutes Drill C, Sixth Reading, 5 Minutes
Sat/Sun	Drill A, Fifth Reading, 5 Minutes Drill B, Seventh Reading, 5 Minutes Drill C, Sixth Reading, 10 Minutes

"Waves"

THE BROKEN CHORD figures in the right hand are to be played legato. The difficulty of this Drill lies in connecting the left and right hands. Make the left hand notes on the first and third beats of each measure sound as if they are connected to the right hand. Imagine a giant arpeggio played by one large hand. If that were possible, such a hand would give you the correct sound for this Drill.

First Reading

Right hand alone. Play the notes of the right hand together as blocked chords, as in the example below. ♩=66-76.

Second Reading

Hands together. Play as written in the example above. ♩=80-88.

Third Reading

Hands together as written. Play legato and *mf.* ♪=100-126.

Fourth Reading

Hands together as written. Play legato and *mf.* ♪=120-144 (♩=60-72).

Fifth Reading

Hands together. Play legato and *mf.* ♩=76-88.

DRILL A

THIS etude combines arpeggios on several different types of chords. Measures 1, 3, 4 and 8 are major chords. Measure 6 is a minor chord; measure 5 is a diminished seventh chord. A dominant seventh chord is used in measures 2 and 7. These different chord types have different "shapes" (patterns on the keyboard) and the notes of each chord consequently have varying spaces between them.

First Reading

Right hand alone. Play legato and *f.* Be careful to follow the fingering exactly as it is notated in the music. ♪=96-112.

Second Reading

Right hand alone. Play legato and *p.* ♪=120-144 (♩=60-72).

Third Reading

Right hand alone. Play legato and *f.* Use the following rhythmic variation:

Each measure in the example above equals one beat of the original. ♩=88-100.

Fourth Reading

Right hand alone. Play legato and *f.* Use the following rhythmic variation:

Each measure in the example above is equal to one beat of the original. ♩=88-100.

Fifth Reading

Right hand alone. Play staccato and *p.* Move up one octave. ♪=152-168.

Sixth Reading

Left hand alone. ♩=66-72.

Seventh Reading

Hands together as written. ♩=66-72.

(Drill on next page)

Drill B

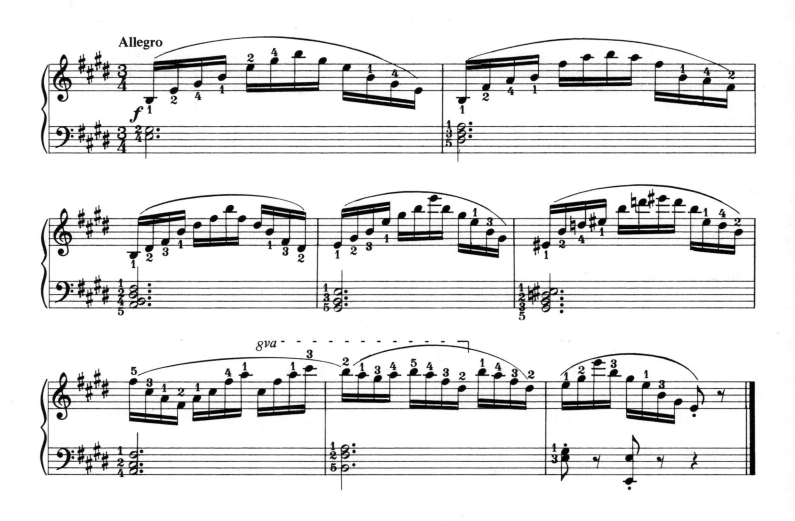

"Darker Shades"

ESSENTIALLY a "mirror" image of the previous drill, this one places the difficulty in the left hand. Only two types of chords are used in this study. Measures 1, 2, 4, 5, 6, and 8 contain major chords. Measures 3 and 7 use dominant seventh chords.

First Reading

Left hand alone. Play legato and *f.* Be careful to follow the fingering exactly as it is notated in the score. ♪=96-112.

Second Reading

Left hand alone. Play legato and *p.* ♪=120-144 (♩=60-72).

Third Reading

Left hand alone. Play legato and *f.* Use the following rhythmic variation:

Each measure in the example above is equal to one beat of the original. ♩=88-100.

Fourth Reading

Left hand alone. Play legato and *f.* Use the following rhythmic variation:

Each measure in the example above is equal to one beat of the original. ♩=88-100.

Fifth Reading

Right hand alone. ♩=66-72.

Sixth Reading

Hands together. ♩=66-72.

(Drill on next page)

Drill C

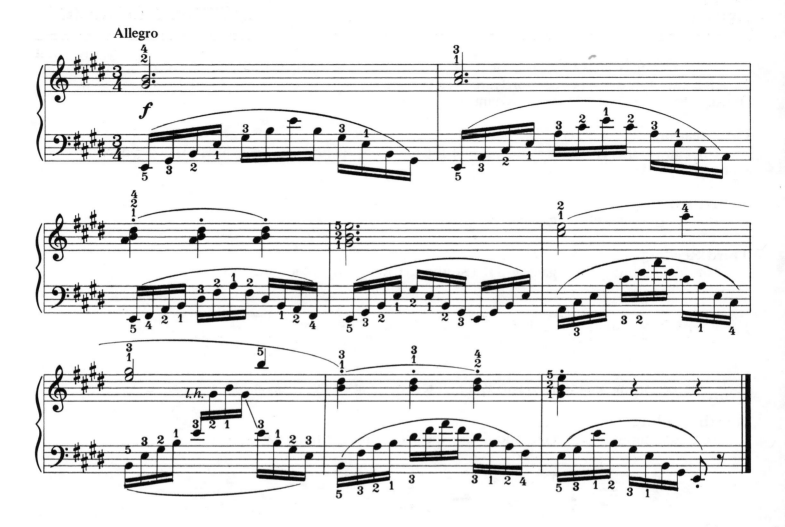

Etude No. 24

Opus 44

Allegro maestoso

BIEHL

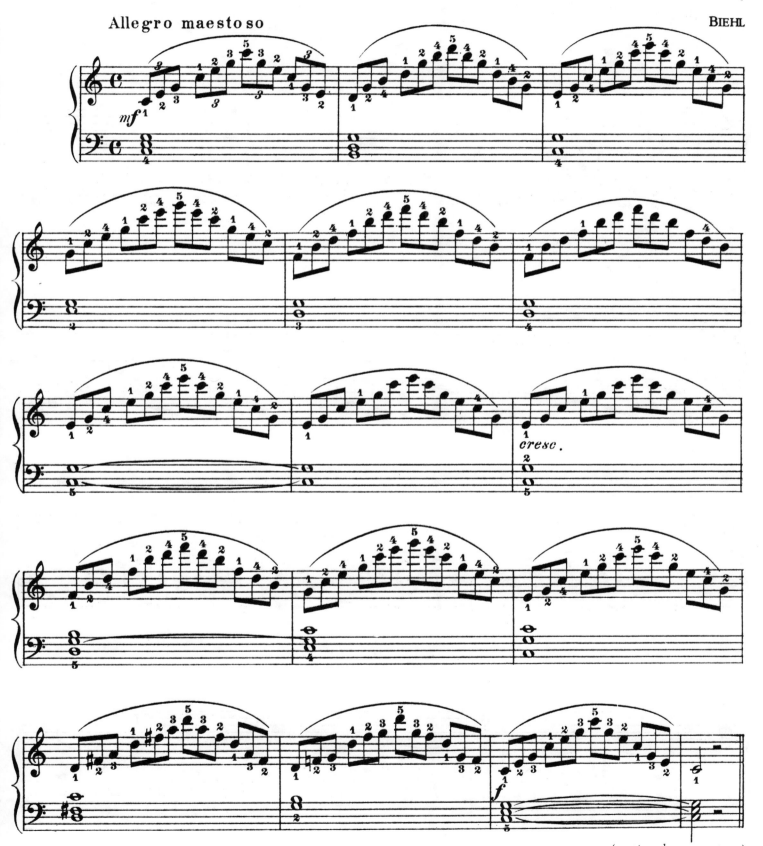

(continued on next page)

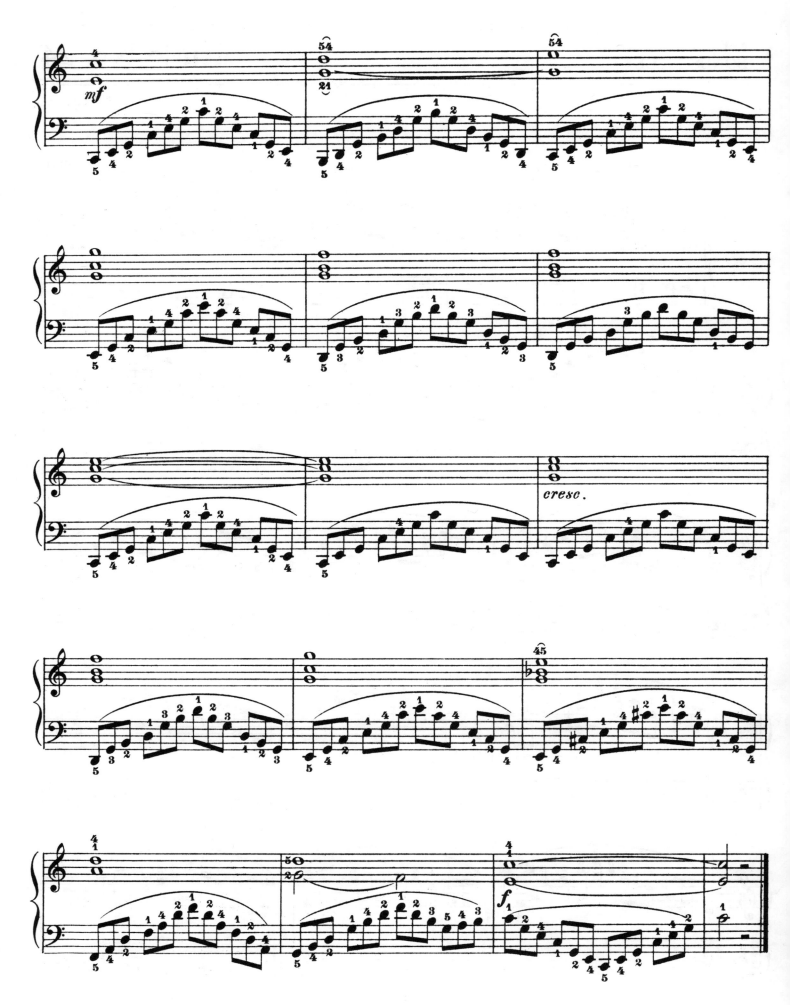

WEEK
15

Monday	Drill A, First Reading, 5 Minutes Drill A, Second Reading, 5 Minutes Drill B, First Reading, 5 Minutes Drill C, First Reading, 5 Minutes
Tuesday	Drill A, Third Reading, 5 Minutes Drill B, Second Reading, 5 Minutes Drill C, First Reading, 5 Minutes Drill C, Second Reading, 5 Minutes
Wednesday	Drill A, Third Reading, 5 Minutes Drill B, Third Reading, 5 Minutes Drill C, Third Reading, 10 Minutes
Thursday	Drill A, Third Reading, 5 Minutes Drill B, Fourth Reading, 5 Minutes Drill C, Fourth Reading, 10 Minutes
Friday	Drill C, Fifth Reading, 5 Minutes Drill C, Sixth Reading, 5 Minutes Drill B, Fifth Reading, 10 Minutes
Sat/Sun	Drill A, Third Reading, 5 Minutes Drill B, Sixth Reading, 5 Minutes Drill C, Sixth Reading, 5 Minutes Drill C, Seventh Reading, 5 Minutes

"Two At A Time"

DRILL A is a duet for one hand. The music is written with two independent parts, or voices. The top voice is notated with the stems going up and the bottom voice has the stems going down. When playing Drill A you should aim to make the piece sound as if it were being played by two different instruments. This is a musical challenge and a technical challenge as well. The half notes of the "melody" (the notes with the stems going up) are to be accented in order to make them stand out over the accompaniment. Since these notes must be held down while you play the eighth notes, be careful not to "squeeze" against the keys. Instead, hold the keys down with as little energy as possible, so that you will be free to play the eighth notes with ease. You will not be able to make every note legato.

First Reading

Play the melody alone, as in the following example. Use the thumb on each note. This is the fingering that you will use when playing both parts together. ♩=80-96.

Second Reading

Play the accompaniment alone, as in the following example. Use the fingering that is written in the music. Not every note will be legato. ♩=80-96.

Third Reading

Play both parts together as written. Accent the half notes and play the eighth notes softly. ♩=80-96.

Drill A

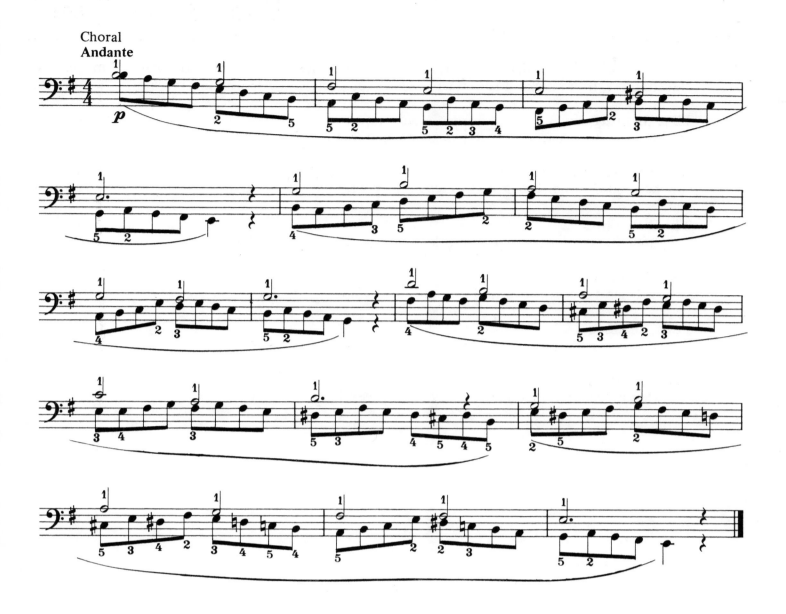

"Four At A Time"

IN CONTRAST to Drill A, this Drill is less of a piece and more of an exercise. Nevertheless, try to make it sound as "musical" as possible when you are playing.

First Reading
Right hand alone. Play *p* and as legato as possible. ♪=108-126.

Second Reading
Left hand alone. Play *p* and as legato as possible. ♪=108-126.

Third Reading
Right hand alone. Play *p* and as legato as possible. ♪=132-160.

Fourth Reading
Left hand alone. Play *p* and as legato as possible. ♪=132-160.

Fifth Reading
Hands together. Play *p* and as legato as possible. ♪=108-126.

Sixth Reading
Hands together. Play *p* and as legato as possible. ♪=132-160.

Drill B

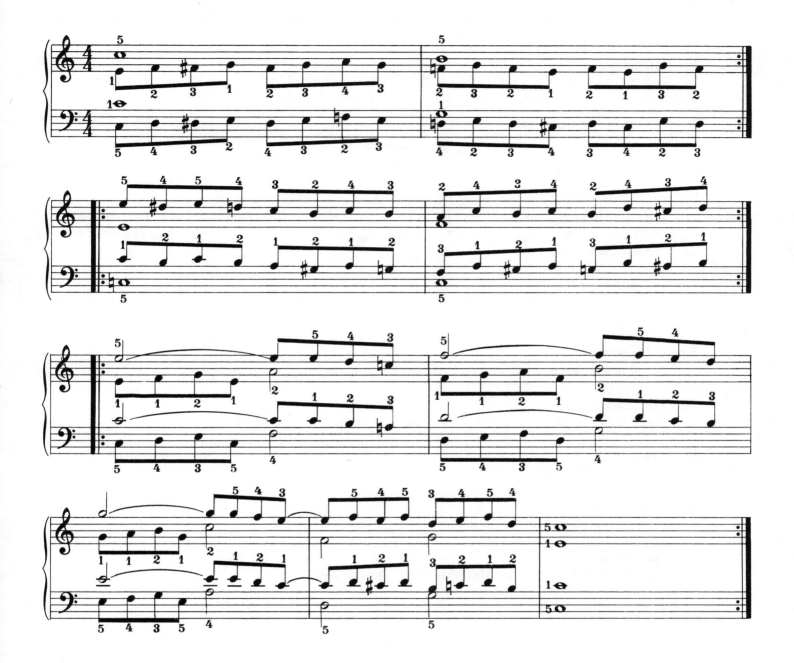

"Three At A Time"

First Reading

Left hand alone. Play legato and use the dynamics marked in the score. Notice that the first notes of measures 1, 2 and 3 are written as both eighth notes and dotted half notes.

Use as little energy as possible in order to keep the dotted half note held down. Do not squeeze against the key. In measures 4, 5, 6 and 7 the first and fourth beats are written both as eighth notes and as dotted quarter notes.

Second Reading

Right hand alone. Play legato and use the dynamics marked in the score. Be certain that you use the fingering marked. ♪=112-132. Each ♪

Third Reading

Right hand alone. Play legato. Increase the tempo to ♪=66-72.

Fourth Reading

Right hand alone. Play legato. Increase the tempo to ♪=84-96.

Fifth Reading

Hands together. ♪=66-72.

Sixth Reading

Hands together. Increase the tempo to ♪=84-96.

Seventh Reading

Hands together. Increase the tempo to ♪=112-144.

Drill C

Consolation

JOHANN BURGMÜLLER

Allegro moderato (♩=152)

WEEK 16

Monday	Drill A, First Reading, 5 Minutes Drill B, First and Second Readings, 5 Minutes Drill C, First Reading, 10 Minutes
Tuesday	Drill A, Second Reading, 5 Minutes Drill B, Third Reading, 5 Minutes Drill C, Second Reading, 10 Minutes
Wednesday	Drill A, Third Reading, 5 Minutes Drill B, Fourth and Fifth Readings, 5 Minutes Drill C, Third Reading, 5 Minutes Drill C, Fourth Reading, 5 Minutes
Thursday	Drill A, Fourth Reading, 5 Minutes Drill B, Fifth Reading, 5 Minutes Drill C, Fifth Reading, 10 Minutes
Friday	Drill A, Fifth Reading, 5 Minutes Drill B, Sixth Reading, 5 Minutes Drill C, Sixth Reading, 5 Minutes Drill C, Seventh Reading, 5 Minutes
Sat/Sun	Drill A, Fifth Reading, 5 Minutes Drill B, Seventh Reading, 5 Minutes Drill C, Eighth Reading, 10 Minutes

"Reaching"

WHEN playing the right hand, remember to allow your wrist and elbow to move freely. Hold down the left hand whole notes as lightly as possible so that you will have enough freedom to play the quarter notes with ease. Each whole note must be held throughout the measure. In measure 7, make certain that you move the left hand in toward the cover of the keyboard in order to play the B*b* with your thumb.

First Reading
Right hand alone. Play legato with the dynamics indicated in the score. ♪=104-116.

Second Reading
Right hand alone. Increase the tempo to ♪=120-144 (♩=60-72).

Third Reading
Left hand alone. Play legato with the dynamics marked in the score. ♩=60-72.

Fourth Reading
Hands together. ♩=60-72.

Fifth Reading
Hands together. Increase the tempo to ♩=80-88.

DRILL A

Drill B is a "quartet" for two hands. Each hand plays two parts. The right hand has a melody on the top:

This melody is combined with an accompaniment below:

The left hand also has two parts. The bass is on the bottom:

This bass is combined with an accompaniment, also in the left hand:

First Reading

Right hand alone. Play the melody without the accompaniment. Play *mf* and use the fingering in the music. You will not make all of the notes legato. ♩=84-100.

Second Reading

Right hand alone. Play the accompaniment without the melody. Play *p* and use the fingering in the music. ♩=84-100.

Third Reading

Right hand alone. Play the right hand as written. Accent the notes of the melody, the first note of each beat. Keep the notes of the accompaniment soft. ♩=84-100.

Fourth Reading

Left hand alone. Play the bass only. Use the fingering in the music. Play *mf.* ♩=84-100.

Fifth Reading

Left hand alone. Play the accompaniment. Use the fingering in the music. Play *mf.* ♩=84-100.

Sixth Reading

Left hand alone. Play the left hand as written. Accent the notes of the bass, the first notes of each measure. Keep the notes of the accompaniment soft. ♩=84-100.

Seventh Reading

Hands together. Make the melody in the right hand predominate over the other parts. ♩=84-100.

(Drill on next page)

Drill B

"Rotations"

THIS IS a difficult Drill because it uses continuous arpeggio figures. Try to achieve a light, clear sound.

First Reading

Right hand alone. Play legato and *f.* Be certain that you are using the fingering marked in the music. ♪=120-132.

Second Reading

Right hand alone. Play legato and *p.* ♪=80-88.

Third Reading

Right hand alone. Play legato and *mf.* ♩=60-72.

Fourth Reading

Left hand alone. Play staccato as marked. ♩=60-72.

Fifth Reading

Hands together. ♩=60-72.

Sixth Reading

Right hand alone. Practice with the following rhythmic variation:

♪=104-116.

Seventh Reading

Right hand alone. Practice with the following rhythmic variation:

♪=104-116.

Eighth Reading

Hands together as written. ♩=80-108.

(Drill on next page)

Drill C

The Clear Stream

JOHANN BURGMÜLLER

WEEK
17

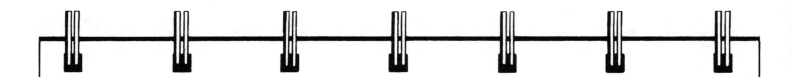

Monday	Drill A, First Reading, 5 Minutes Drill B, First Reading, 5 Minutes Drill C, First Reading, 5 Minutes Drill D, First Reading, 5 Minutes
Tuesday	Drill A, Second Reading, 5 Minutes Drill B, Second Reading, 5 Minutes Drill C, Second Reading, 5 Minutes Drill C, Third Reading, 5 Minutes
Wednesday	Drill D, First Reading, 5 Minutes Drill A, Third Reading, 5 Minutes Drill B, Third Reading, 10 Minutes
Thursday	Drill C, Fourth Reading, 10 Minutes Drill D, Second Reading, 5 Minutes Drill B, Fourth Reading, 5 Minutes
Friday	Drill A, Fourth Reading, 5 Minutes Drill B, Fifth Reading, 5 Minutes Drill C, Fifth Reading, 5 Minutes Drill D, Third Reading, 5 Minutes
Sat/Sun	Drill A, Fourth Reading, 5 Minutes Drill B, Fifth Reading, 5 Minutes Drill C, Fifth Reading, 5 Minutes Drill D, Third Reading, 5 Minutes

DRILL A

"Seeing Double"

DOUBLE notes—two or more notes played at the same time—such as those in the following Drill, can be repeated by using a wrist motion when they are staccato. Unlike single repeated notes, which you may repeat by changing fingers, the thirds and sixths in this study can only be played by letting your wrist move freely.

First Reading
Right hand alone. Play staccato and legato as marked. Follow the dynamics. ♪=104-120.

Second Reading
Right hand alone. Increase the tempo to ♪=144-160.

Third Reading
Left hand alone. Play staccato and *p.* ♩=72-80.

Fourth Reading
Hands together. ♩=88-96.

DRILL A

"Strumming"

IMAGINE that the left hand of this Drill is being performed by string instruments played pizzicato (with plucked strings). At the same time try to make the right hand melody sound as if it were played by a wind instrument, such as a flute or oboe.

First Reading
Left hand alone. Play *p* and staccato. ♪=96-112.

Second Reading
Right hand alone. Play *mf* and legato. ♪=96-112.

Third Reading
Hands together. Play the right hand *mf* and legato. Play the left hand *p* and staccato. ♪=96-112.

Fourth Reading
Hands together. Play the right hand *mf* and legato. Play the left hand *p* and staccato. ♪=120-144.

Fifth Reading
Hands together. Play the right hand *mf* and legato. Play the left hand *p* and staccato. ♪=152-168.

DRILL B

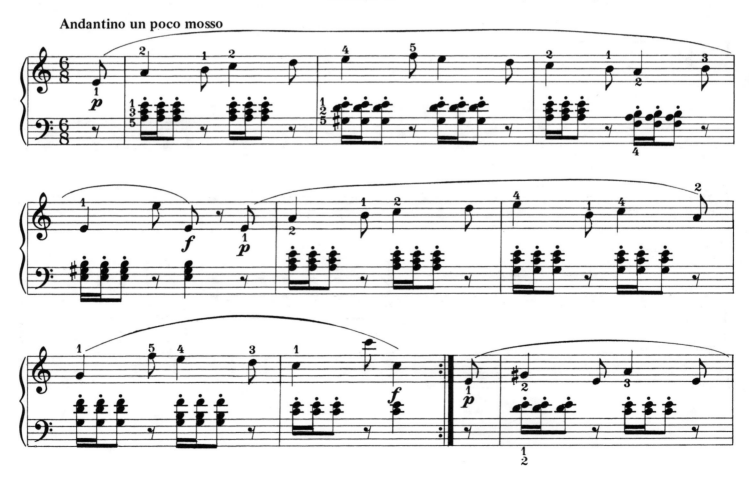

Andantino un poco mosso

"Third Bass"

LEGATO thirds set against a staccato accompaniment require independence of the hands in this Etude by Czerny. Because the thirds in the right hand are played by different pairs of fingers, it is not difficult to achieve a legato sound. There is one exception: in measures 26 and 27. The bottom note of the last beat of measure 26 and the bottom note of the first beat of measure 27 must be played with the thumb. Consequently it is not possible to connect these two notes.

It is still possible, however, to make these notes sound as if they were legato. Hold down the top note, the A, of the last beat in measure 26, while lifting the bottom note, the F. Connect the A to the G, on the first beat of the following measure, and move the thumb from the F, the last beat of measure 26, to the E, the first beat of measure 27. Although the bottom notes of these thirds are not played legato, we tend to hear the two pairs as though they were, due to the legato movement of the top notes.

First Reading
Right hand alone. Play legato and staccato as marked. ♩=80-96.

Second Reading
Left hand alone. Play staccato and **p.** ♩=80-96.

Third Reading
Left hand alone. Play all three notes of the measure as a blocked chord. Example:

♩=80-96.

Fourth Reading
Hands together. Play as written. ♩=80-96.

Fifth Reading
Hands together. Increase the tempo to ♩=100-120.

Drill C

"In Third Gear"

First Reading
Play legato with the exception of the last pair of notes of each triplet. Do not connect these notes to the following notes. Although they are marked staccato, in this case the marking does not indicate that the notes are to be played short, but that they are not to be connected to the following notes. ♪=120-132.

Second Reading
Move the hand down one octave. ♪=144-160.

Third Reading
Move the hand up one octave. ♪=160-184.

DRILL D

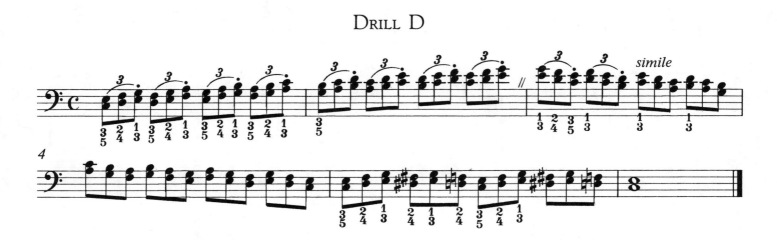

Recurrences

JOHANN BURGMÜLLER

(continued on next page)

132

WEEK 18

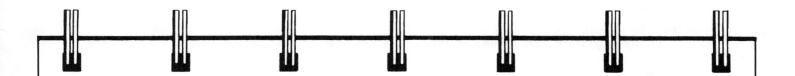

Monday	Drill A, First Reading, 5 Minutes Drill A, Second Reading, 5 Minutes Drill C, First Reading, 5 Minutes Drill D, First Reading, 5 Minutes
Tuesday	Drill B, First Reading, 5 Minutes Drill B, Second Reading, 5 Minutes Drill C, Second Reading, 5 Minutes Drill D, Second Reading, 5 Minutes
Wednesday	Drill A, Third Reading, 5 Minutes Drill B, Third Reading, 5 Minutes Drill C, Second Reading, 5 Minutes Drill D, Third Reading, 5 Minutes
Thursday	Drill D, Fourth Reading, 10 Minutes Drill A, Fourth Reading, 5 Minutes Drill B, Fourth Reading, 5 Minutes Drill C, Third Reading, 5 Minutes
Friday	Drill D, Fifth Reading, 5 Minutes Drill C, Fourth Reading, 5 Minutes Drill B, Fifth Reading, 5 Minutes Drill A, Fifth Reading, 5 Minutes
Sat/Sun	Drill A, Fifth Reading, 5 Minutes Drill B, Fifth Reading, 5 Minutes Drill C, Fourth Reading, 5 Minutes Drill D, Fifth Reading, 5 Minutes

"Pumping Ivory"

WHEN playing double notes be certain that both notes sound simultaneously in each hand. Because most of the notes in these two Drills are to be played legato, almost no wrist motion is necessary. Follow the same directions for both A and B.

First Reading
Right hand alone. Play legato and *mp.* ♪=104-120.

Second Reading
Left hand alone. Play legato and *mp.* ♪=104-120.

Third Reading
Hands together. Play legato and *mp.* ♪=104-120.

Fourth Reading
Hands together. Play legato and *mp.* Increase the tempo to ♪=132-144 (♩=66-72).

Fifth Reading
Hands together. Move both hands up one octave. Play legato and *f.* Increase the tempo to ♩=80-88.

DRILL A

"Smooth Moves"

THERE is one difficult legato connection in this piece. The last pair of thirds in measure 1 should be connected to the first pair of measure 2. Because the third finger must be used for the bottom note of the first pair and the top note of the second pair, it is impossible to connect both notes of the two pairs. In order to make them sound as if they were legato, release the bottom note, G, of the last third in measure 1, but hold down the top note of this pair, which should be connected to the *bottom* note of the first third of the following measure. Example:

Notice that you must do the same thing between measures 3 and 4, 5 and 6, 7 and 8, etc.

First Reading
Play legato and *mp.* ♪=112-132.

Second Reading
Play legato and *f.* ♪=144-168.

Third Reading
Play legato and *p.* Move the hand down one octave. ♩=80-88.

Fourth Reading
Play as written. ♩=92-100.

DRILL C

"All Together"

First Reading

Right hand alone, measures 1-16. Left hand alone, measures 17-24. Right hand alone, measures 25-32. Play legato and staccato as marked. ♩=80-92.

Second Reading

Left hand alone, measures 1-16. Right hand alone, measures 17-24. Right hand alone, measures 25-32. Play staccato. ♩=82-92.

Third Reading

Left hand alone, measures 1-16. Right hand alone, measures 17-24. Right hand alone, measures 25-32. Play all of the notes in each measure together as chords. ♩=112-120. Example:

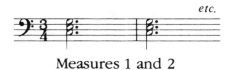

Measures 1 and 2

Measures 17, 18 and 19.

Fourth Reading

Hands together as written. ♩=80-92.

Fifth Reading

Hands together as written. Increase the tempo to ♩=100-112.

(Drill on next page)

DRILL D

Scherzetto

GIUSEPPE CONCONE

(continued on next page)

140

Week 19

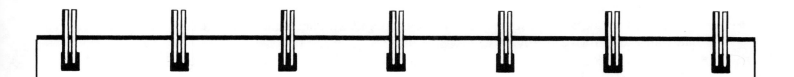

Monday	Drill A, First Reading, 5 Minutes Drill A, Second Reading, 5 Minutes Drill B, First Reading, 5 Minutes Drill C, First Reading, 5 Minutes
Tuesday	Drill C, First Reading, 5 Minutes Drill C, Second Reading, 5 Minutes Drill B, Second Reading, 5 Minutes Drill A, Third Reading, 5 Minutes
Wednesday	Drill A, Fifth Reading, 5 Minutes Drill B, Fourth Reading, 5 Minutes Drill C, Fifth Reading, 10 Minutes
Thursday	Drill A, Fifth Reading, 5 Minutes Drill B, Third Reading, 5 Minutes Drill C, Third Reading, 5 Minutes Drill C, Fourth Reading, 5 Minutes
Friday	Drill A, Second Reading, 5 Minutes Drill B, Fourth Reading, 5 Minutes Drill C, Fifth Reading, 10 Minutes
Sat/Sun	Drill A, Sixth Reading, 10 Minutes Drill B, Fourth Reading, 5 Minutes Drill C, Fifth Reading, 5 Minutes

"At The Top"

RUSSIAN composer Dmitri Kabalevsky combines scale-like figures and arpeggios together in this Etude. With the exception of measures 9-12 where the hands play in unison (both hands playing the same note separated by an octave), the other parts of the piece require complete independence of the hands.

First Reading

Right hand alone, measures 1-8 and measures 13-21. Play legato and staccato as marked. Let your hand and arm move freely to follow the fingers. ♩=72-80.

Second Reading

Left hand alone, measures 1-8 and measures 13-21. Play legato and staccato as marked. Let your hand and arm move freely to follow the fingers. ♩=72-80.

Third Reading

Hands together, measures 9-12. ♩=72-80.

Fourth Reading

Hands together, measures 1-21. Play legato and staccato as marked. ♩=72-80.

Fifth Reading

Hands together. ♩=92-104.

Sixth Reading

Hands together. Increase the tempo to ♩=112-120.

DRILL A

DRILL B combines repeated octaves and double notes. Although the notes are not marked staccato, you cannot connect any of them. Repeated octaves and double notes do not require much finger action. You cannot "pull up" the keys with your fingers. Let your wrist be free and flexible in order to repeat them.

First Reading
Left hand alone. Play non-legato (separated, but neither staccato nor legato) and *mf.* ♪=108-120.

Second Reading
Left hand alone. Play non-legato and *mf.* ♪=126-144.

Third Reading
Left hand alone. Play non-legato and *mf.* ♪=152-168. Move your hand down one octave.

Fourth Reading
Left hand alone as written. Play non-legato and *mf.* ♩=76-84.

DRILL B

"Alternating Current"

WIECK passes chords and octaves back and forth between the hands in this Drill. Notice that the second note in the left hand of measure 16 is F**×** (F double sharp). It is played the same as G. For theoretical reasons, this note must be written as a version of F rather than G.

First Reading

Left hand alone. Play non-legato and *mf.* Use the fourth finger on most of the black key octaves as marked. ♩=92-104.

Second Reading

Right hand alone. Play non-legato and *mf.* Although the notes in the right hand are written on the second half of each beat, practice them on the beat. For example:

♩=92-104.

Third Reading

Hands together as written. Play non-legato and *mf.* ♪=108-116.

Fourth Reading

Hands together. Play non-legato and *mf.* ♪=132-152.

Fifth Reading

Hands together. Play non-legato and *mf.* ♩=80-88.

(Drill on next page)

Drill C

Song Without Words

Opus 102, No. 3

FELIX MENDELSSOHN-BARTHOLDY

(continued on next page)

WEEK
20

Monday	Drill A, First Reading, 5 Minutes Drill B, First Reading, 5 Minutes Drill C, First Reading, 5 Minutes Drill C, Third Reading, 5 Minutes
Tuesday	Drill A, Second Reading, 5 Minutes Drill B, Second Reading, 5 Minutes Drill C, Second Reading, 5 Minutes Drill C, Third Reading, 5 Minutes
Wednesday	Drill C, Third Reading, 5 Minutes Drill C, Fourth Reading, 5 Minutes Drill A, Third Reading, 5 Minutes Drill A, Fourth Reading, 5 Minutes
Thursday	Drill C, Fifth Reading, 10 Minutes Drill B, Third Reading, 5 Minutes Drill A, Fifth Reading, 5 Minutes
Friday	Drill A, Fifth Reading, 5 Minutes Drill B, Fourth Reading, 5 Minutes Drill B, Fifth Reading, 5 Minutes Drill C, Sixth Reading, 5 Minutes
Sat/Sun	Drill A, Sixth Reading, 5 Minutes Drill B, Sixth Reading, 5 Minutes Drill C, Sixth Reading, 10 Minutes

"Octave Passage"

DRILL A combines diatonic (white key) and chromatic (mixed black and white key) octaves. Remember that on black keys the octave is often played with the fourth finger rather than the fifth. The sign *"8va bassa"* indicates that you are to play the notes one octave lower than written.

First Reading
Right hand alone. Play *mp.* ♪=116-132.

Second Reading
Left hand alone. Play *mp.* ♪=116-132.

Third Reading
Right hand alone. Play *f* and staccato. ♪=144-168.

Fourth Reading
Left hand alone. Play *f* and staccato. ♪=144-168.

Fifth Reading
Hands together. Play *p* and staccato. ♩=72-84.

Sixth Reading
Hands together. Play *mp* and staccato. ♩=84-96.

DRILL A

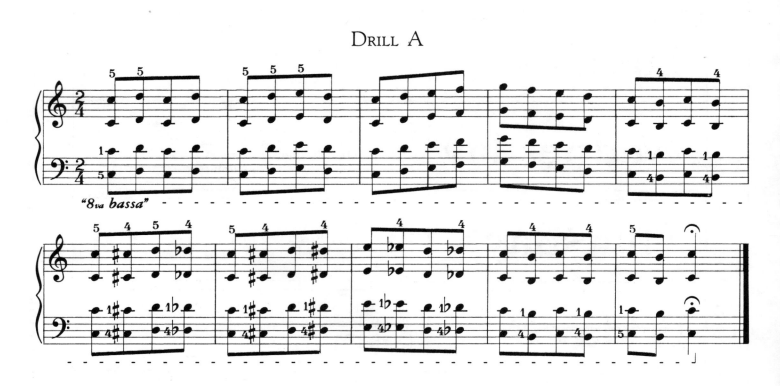

"Contrary Motion"

A STUDY in octaves played in contrary motion (hands going in the opposite direction), Drill B is not too difficult to play since the hands "match" each other. Both hands move in half-steps from one note to the next. Notice that in measure 4 and measure 10 it appears in the music that the notes shift a considerable distance from each other, but remember to look at the *8va* and *8va bassa* signs. Because of these signs the notes are notated in a different octave from the one where they are played on the keyboard. Thus, they continue the half-step progression from one note to the next.

First Reading
 Right hand alone. Play legato and *mf.* ♪=112-126.

Second Reading
 Left hand alone. Play legato and *mf.* ♪=112-126.

Third Reading
 Hands together. Play legato and *mf.* ♪=112-126.

Fourth Reading
 Hands together. Play staccato and *p.* ♪=112-126.

Fifth Reading
 Hands together. Play staccato and *f.* ♪=144-160.

Sixth Reading
 Hands together. Play legato and *mf.* ♩=76-88.

DRILL B

"Final Study"

IN ORDER to play this Drill well you must have control over each of the hands separately. The left hand is the accompaniment and you must know it solidly so that you will be able to focus your attention on the right hand.

First Reading

Left hand alone. Play *p*. ♩ =66-76.

Second Reading

Left hand alone. Play *p*. ♩ =84-88.

Third Reading

Right hand alone. Play *p* and staccato. The staccato dots are not indicated over each octave, but the indication "stacc." in measure 2 tells you that you are to continue to play staccato throughout the Drill. Remember that in this Drill three eighth notes equal one quarter note. In this case the eighth notes are triplets (♪♪♪ = ♩). ♩ =66-76.

Fourth Reading

Right hand alone. Play *p* and staccato. ♩ =84-88.

Fifth Reading

Hands together. Play *p* and staccato. ♩ =66-76.

Sixth Reading

Hands together. Play *p* and staccato. ♩ =84-88.

Drill C

Octave Etude

THEODORE KULLAK

The Book Musicians Are Raving About!

KEYBOARD TRICKS OF THE TRADE

Over 350 Pages!

- The Most Complete Book of Self-Instruction!
- For Pianists, Organists, All Keyboard Players!
- Includes Numerous Charts and Illustrations!

If you are the kind of keyboard player, pianist or organist who wants to get MORE out of your music . . . if you think your playing is in a rut . . . or wish someone would explain keyboard theory and harmony to you in easy-to-understand terms . . . if you'd like to spice up your playing with some of the tricks the professionals use . . . in short, if you want to improve your playing and understanding of music dramatically . . . THIS BOOK IS FOR YOU!

Be A Better Musician!

Here is the kind of book you can pick up at any page and learn something new. You can use it as a handy reference guide to solve musical problems, or as a browser's manual to pick up valuable bits and pieces of information it might take weeks to find in a library.

Take the section on chords, for example. You get a complete catalog of every possible keyboard chord, plus picture chords in easy-to-read keyboard diagrams. It's a virtual encyclopedia of all the chords used in pop music, graphically illustrated so everyone can easily understand them. In addition, there are complete sections on *rhythm* — how to play it, how to read it with ease — *finger speed and dexterity . . . creating and imitating keyboard styles* . . . theory and improvisation . . . an entire "organ only" section, plus much, much more.

Teachers Love it

Teachers! Now you can give your students the kind of supplemental reading they need to speed their comprehension and progress along at record pace. It's the perfect kind of *fun* book to pique students' interest and get them more deeply involved with their music.

Money Back If Not Delighted

Keep this book for a full 30 days. If after that time you are not completely thrilled and delighted with all that it has to offer, if you do not agree that it is everything we say it is, then simply return it to us for a full and prompt refund.

No questions asked.

So hurry and order yours TODAY!

● ● ● ● ● ● ● ● ● ● ● ● ● ● ● ● ● ●

HOW TO ORDER

Write down on any piece of paper the number of copies of "Keyboard Tricks Of The Trade" you want. Print your name and address, including zip code. For each copy, enclose check or money order for $19.95 plus $2.00 postage and handling payable to Songbooks Unlimited. (N.Y. & N.J. residents add sales tax.) Mail to SONGBOOKS UNLIMITED, Dept. TR-01-18, 352 Evelyn St., P.O. Box 908, Paramus, NJ 07653-0908. We will ship promptly with full 30 day money back guarantee.

Read Music From Broadway To Bach At Sight...

Speed-Reading At The Keyboard

Speed-Reading At The Keyboard

By Edward Shanaphy, Stuart Isacoff and Julie Jordan

Volume 1

- **A Complete Course In Three Giant Volumes!**
- **For Keyboard Players Of All Levels!**
- **Just 20 Minutes A Day!**

Speed-Reading At The Keyboard

By Edward Shanaphy, Stuart Isacoff and Julie Jordan

Volume 2

Speed-Reading At The Keyboard

By Edward Shanaphy, Stuart Isacoff and Julie

Volume 3

Supplemental Volume *Reading Accompani*

A 20% Savings!

Most musicians share a common dream: to be able to play *at sight* any sheet music placed in front of them — no matter what style or level of difficulty. Imagine being able to breeze through the latest pop song, or a favorite Broadway overture . . . or even one of the great classical themes — even if you've never seen it before!

A few musicians with this remarkable ability have proved it can be done. But no teacher or course has ever been available to pass along the *trade secrets* of this very special art. Until now!!

Sight-Reading Secrets

For the first time ever, here is a spectacular achievement in the field of music education . . . a complete three-volume course guaranteed to help any keyboard player master the art of sight-reading! It teaches you, step-by-step, how to recognize musical phrases, rhythms and harmonies *at a glance*. Go at your own pace as you follow the daily routines outlined in the *Speed-Reading* course. As little as 20 minutes a day will train your musical reflexes to make you a better sight-reader than you ever thought possible!

Half The Fun Is Getting There

The most important part of becoming a good sight-reader is to play as many kinds of music as possible. That's why, when you receive SPEED-READING AT THE KEYBOARD, you also get over 200 pieces to play. (By itself, this collection is a fantastic library of music to own.) In addition to receiving all this music, you will learn, piece by piece, from the very simple to the complex, exactly how to master the art of playing it at sight.

All of the music you receive with SPEED-READING AT THE KEYBOARD has been specially sequenced to ensure a logically graduated progression. And the best part is that the pieces are all fun to play.

There are examples from every style of music . . from beautiful waltzes, operettas and operas, themes from great concertos, folk music, and popular melodies to piano favorites of the masters. You will find a lilting Scott Joplin Rag next to a delicate Mozart minuet, a Strauss waltz followed by a soaring romantic theme. As you master each section of this three-volume course you will be amazed to find that you are reading music (on the spot!) better than you had ever imagined possible.

Special Savings!

Purchased separately, these three volumes would cost over $50, but through this special limited time introductory offer you pay just $39.95 — a savings of over 20%!

Unconditional Guarantee!

Keep this course for 30 days — use it, play the music it contains, study its principles. If for any reason you are not thrilled and delighted with the course, and with your own improvement, we will gladly refund the full purchase price. So hurry and order your copy today. *You have absolutely nothing to lose!*

★ ★ ★ HOW TO ORDER ★ ★ ★

Write down on any piece of paper your name and address, including zip code. Enclose a check or money order for just $39.95 plus $2.95 postage and handling for the complete three-volume SPEED-READING AT THE KEYBOARD. (Make checks payable to Songbooks Unlimited. N.Y. and N.J. residents add sales tax.) Or, CHARGE IT. Include your MasterCard or VISA account number and expiration date. Mail to SONGBOOKS UNLIMITED, Dept. SR-01-18, 352 Evelyn St., P.O. Box 908, Paramus, NJ 07653-0908. If you're not completely delighted, you may return the course within 30 days for a full refund.